GW00674963

AIRCRAFT
ARCHIVE

AIRCRAFT OF WORLD WAR ONE

VOLUME 2

Argus Books
Wolsey House
Wolsey Road
Hemel Hempstead
Herts. HP2 4SS
England

First published by Argus Books 1989

ISBN 0 85242 984 3

Designed by Little Oak Studios
Phototypesetting by Typesetters (Birmingham) Ltd
Printed and bound in Great Britain by
William Clowes Limited, Beccles and London

Cover photo: Colourful Fokker D VII 286/18 airborne over
upper New York State where Cole Palen retains his unique
collection at Old Rhinebeck. Once the property of Bert
Acosta who flew Cdr Byrd's *America* Fokker Trimotor across
the Atlantic a month after Lindbergh, this D VII is a rare
flying example.

AIRCRAFT ARCHIVE

AIRCRAFT OF WORLD WAR ONE

VOLUME 2

Contents

Introduction 4

Great Britain
Bristol F2B 6
De Havilland DH2 12
Royal Aircraft Factory BE2c 16
Royal Aircraft Factory FE2b 20
Royal Aircraft Factory SE5 and SE5a 24
Sopwith Buffalo 29
Sopwith F1 Camel 32

France
Maurice Farman Shorthorn 35
Morane Saulnier Type L 39
Nieuport 11 42
Nieuport 24 and 27 45
SPAD VII 47

Belgium
Hanriot HD1 49

Germany
Albatros B I 52
Albatros B II and IIa 55
Albatros C V/16 and 17 60
Albatros D III 64
Albatros J I 67
Albatros J II 69
DFW C V 71
Fokker D VII 75
Fokker Dr 1 78
Gotha G IV and V 80
LVG C VI 88
Roland D II 92
Rumpler C IV 94

A DETAILED COLLECTION OF ORIGINAL SCALE AIRCRAFT DRAWINGS

Introduction

When the first squadrons flew to the British Expeditionary Force at Amiens from Dover – an achievement commemorated by the Dover RFC Memorial – they were venturing into the very beginning of aerial combat. The date was 13 August 1914, the aircraft a miscellany of unarmed Farmans, plus BE2s soon to be fitted in the field with guns and 'flechettes'. It took a full year before the advanced BE2c and protective Bristol Scouts arrived, but 1915 saw the start of accelerated aeronautical development which led eventually to the efficient scout-fighter and multi-engined bomber.

Engines, rotary or liquid cooled in-line, took their own toll whenever the Claudel-Hobson carburettors coughed to stifle critical power after take-off, and spares had to be foraged wherever possible. Very little has been written of the air mechanics who bore the brunt of front-line attacks, living by their wits and coping with endless repairs from tailskids to propellers. Among them, James McCudden, who went to France with No 3 Squadron as a 2nd Class Air Mechanic, became a sergeant pilot on DH2s within the year, and as Major J T B McCudden VC DSO MC MM was a victim of engine failure in his SE5a on 9 July 1918 after 57 victories.

The war ended with many other fighting heroes – Guynemeyer, Immelmann, Boelke, Udet, Ball, Bishop, Mannock and von Richthofen, whose exploits were recounted vividly in the editions of *Air Stories, Popular Flying* and *Flying Aces*. Fiction added to the lustre of these fighting pilots: we owe to much to W E John's fictional 'Captain James Biggles' and Donald Keyhoe's 'Philip Strange', and to the thrilling personal stories by Arch Whitehouse and Joe Archibald. Illustrators Stanley Orton Bradshaw and Howard Leigh recaptured air battle scenes while still fresh in the memory, and those scale drawing pioneers Leonard Bridgeman and James Hay Stevens made accurate models possible for the first time.

Parallel with the publishers were those rare British individuals Richard Shuttleworth and R G J Nash, who sought to preserve WWI aeroplanes for posterity. It is thanks to them that visitors to the Shuttleworth Collection and the Royal Air Force Museum can gaze upon the actual hardware, restored to perfection and, in the case of Shuttleworth, in flying condition.

Now a fresh surge of interest in World War I arises with a plethora of new model kits and special publications. Leon Opdyke's *World War One Aero* and Ray Rimell's *Windsock International* contain a wealth of detail with each new edition. They show how so much still remains to be discovered – even 75 years after the event! Much of their material will supplement the contents of this volume, which makes no pretence at being 'the last word' on WWI aeroplanes.

◄ Three Bristol F2Bs of 39 (Home Defence) Squadron with the white elements removed from all markings, while, to confuse, the blue appears as white! (J M Bruce/G S Leslie)

◀ Rare treat for present day WWI enthusiasts, and a regular scene at Old Warden pageants: the Shuttleworth LVG C VI, Bristol Fighter and SE5a in formation over Bedfordshire. (R Moulton)

The following pages carry reprints of 1/72nd scale drawings that appeared in *Aeromodeller* and *Scale Models* over the period from 1950 to 1983. They form a representative collection of work by specialists who introduced new standards of fine-detail draughting. Each has his own style, and all have the same aim – to record with accuracy the shapes and structures of aeroplanes that have in the majority of cases disappeared forever. It is to Maurice Brett, Peter Cooksley, George Cox, Peter Gray, Eddie Riding, Ian Stair and Harry Woodman that we owe gratitude for the research which enabled them to establish these scale views.

Equally, we are indebted to the photo collections which are credited with each caption. In particular, without the help of Jack Bruce, Alex Imrie, Stuart Leslie, Ray Rimell and Harry Woodman the 100-plus illustrations and their informative descriptions simply would not have been possible. Publishing files are seldom complete after as much as 30 years of storage, and such was the scarcity of original photographs that many had been returned to authors after first appearance in the magazine. Fortunately, friendships which had formed through a mutual enthusiasm for the subject overcame many hurdles and ensured the selection which the reader can now enjoy in this and the companion Volume 1 of the series.

Albatros D Va and Fokker Dr 1 triplanes of *Jagdstaffel 12* lined up on Toulis aerodrome near Laon, March 1918. All machines have with the unit identification markings of white nose and black tail unit, the personal markings of pilots being carried on the fuselage sides. (A Imrie)
▼

Bristol F2B

Country of origin: Great Britain.
Type: Two-seat fighter-reconnaissance aircraft.
Powerplant: One Rolls-Royce Falcon I twelve-cylinder, liquid-cooled engine rated at 190hp, Falcon II rated at 220hp, Falcon III rated at 275hp, Sunbeam Arab rated at 200hp or Hispano-Suiza rated at 200hp.
Dimensions: Wing span 39ft 4in *12.09m*, (Hispano) 39ft 3in *11.96m*; length 26ft 2in *7.98m*, (Hispano) 24ft 9in *7.54m*; height 10ft 1in *3.07m*, (Hispano) 9ft 6in *2.90m*; wing area 406 sq ft *37.72m²*, (Hispano) 405 sq ft *37.62m²*.
Weights: Empty 1745lb *791kg*, (Hispano, Sunbeam) 1733lb *786kg*; loaded 2590lb *1175kg*, (Hispano, Sunbeam) 2630lb *1193kg*.
Performance: Maximum speed 125mph *201kph* at sea level, (Hispano, Sunbeam) 105mph *169kph* at 10,000ft *3050m*; time to 6500ft *1980m*, 6.5min, (Hispano, Sunbeam) 8.7min; service ceiling 20,000ft *6100m*, (Hispano, Sunbeam) 19,000ft *5485m*; endurance 3hr.
Armament: One fixed Vickers machine gun and one or two flexibly mounted Lewis machine guns, plus up to twelve 20lb *9kg* bombs.
Service: First flight (modified F2A) late 1916; service entry June 1917.

Port elevation, Mk I
▼

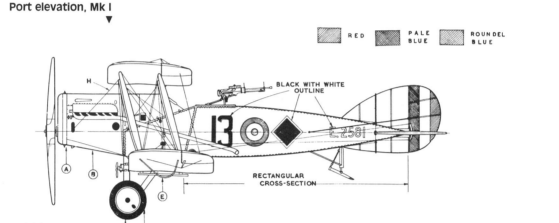

RED   PALE BLUE   ROUNDEL BLUE

BLACK WITH WHITE OUTLINE

RECTANGULAR CROSS-SECTION

SHORT EXHAUST ON SOME MACHINES

With its tall, pencil-box style radiators beside the fuselage, the Bristol F2A prototype A3303 had a Rolls-Royce Falcon I engine. Pilot vision was obscured by the radiators, resulting in the circular nose radiator which was to become standard. (Bristol)
▼

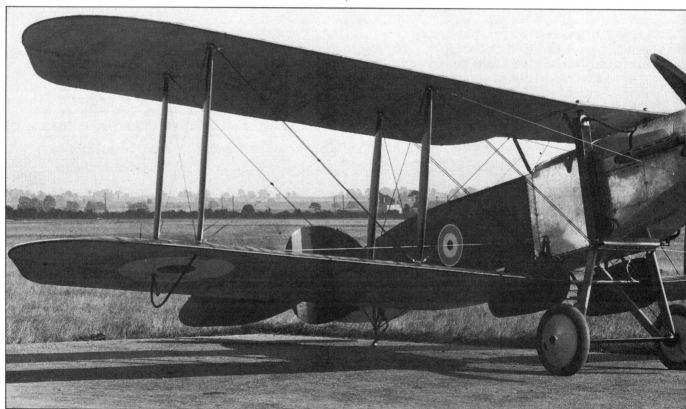

▲ Postwar Mk IV versions with wing slats and horn-balanced rudders, in service with the Cambridge University Air Squadron. (C E Brown)

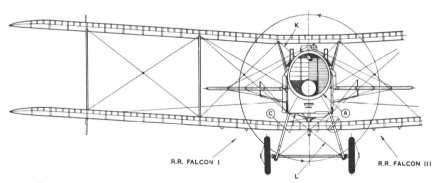

R.R. FALCON I   R.R. FALCON III

▲ Front elevation, Mk I
Starboard side

▲ Front elevation, Mk IV
Port side

◄ Fuselage cross-sections

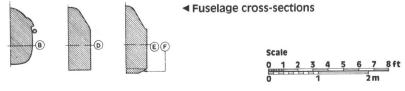

Scale

0 1 2 3 4 5 6 7 8 ft

0   1   2 m

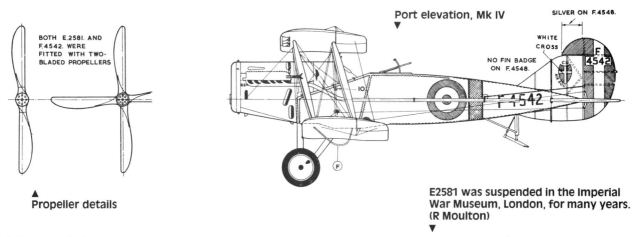

BOTH E.2581. AND F.4542. WERE FITTED WITH TWO-BLADED PROPELLERS

▲ Propeller details

Port elevation, Mk IV ▼

SILVER ON F.4548.

WHITE CROSS

NO FIN BADGE ON F.4548.

F 4542

F.4542

E2581 was suspended in the Imperial War Museum, London, for many years. (R Moulton) ▼

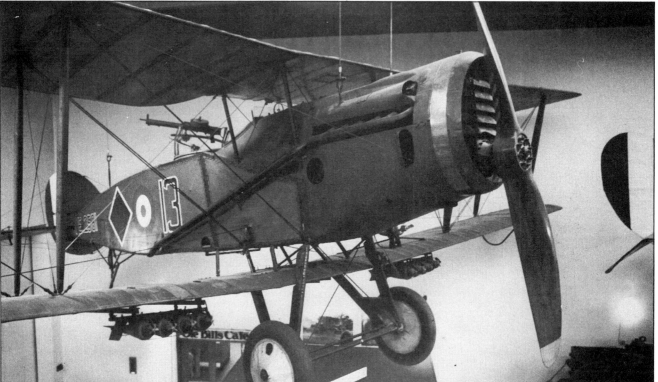

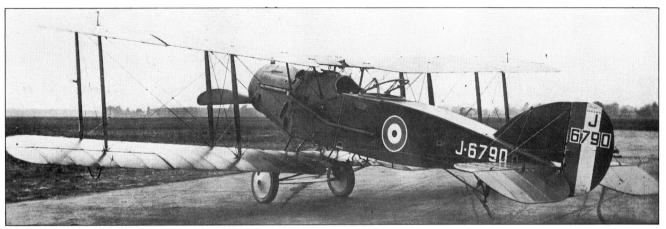

One of the late F2Bs, built by Bristol and Colonial, with the RR Falcon III. (IWM Q67630)

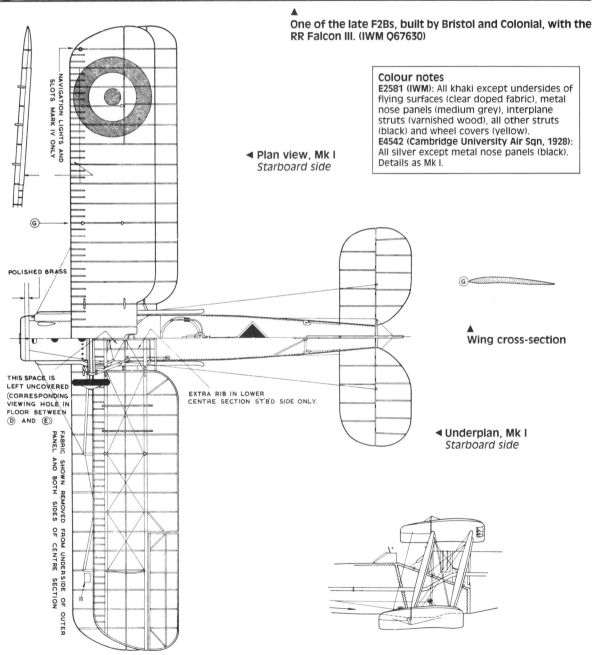

NAVIGATION LIGHTS AND SLOTS MARK IV ONLY

POLISHED BRASS

THIS SPACE IS LEFT UNCOVERED (CORRESPONDING VIEWING HOLE IN FLOOR BETWEEN (D) AND (E)

FABRIC SHOWN REMOVED FROM UNDERSIDE OF OUTER PANEL AND BOTH SIDES OF CENTRE SECTION

◄ Plan view, Mk I
Starboard side

EXTRA RIB IN LOWER CENTRE SECTION ST'B'D SIDE ONLY.

◄ Underplan, Mk I
Starboard side

Colour notes
E2581 (IWM): All khaki except undersides of flying surfaces (clear doped fabric), metal nose panels (medium grey), interplane struts (varnished wood), all other struts (black) and wheel covers (yellow).
E4542 (Cambridge University Air Sqn, 1928): All silver except metal nose panels (black). Details as Mk I.

▲ Wing cross-section

▲ Scrap starboard elevation
F4548 trainer

◄ Airborne over the Avon, the F2B is seen on test after its winter overhaul, 5 April 1957. (Bristol)

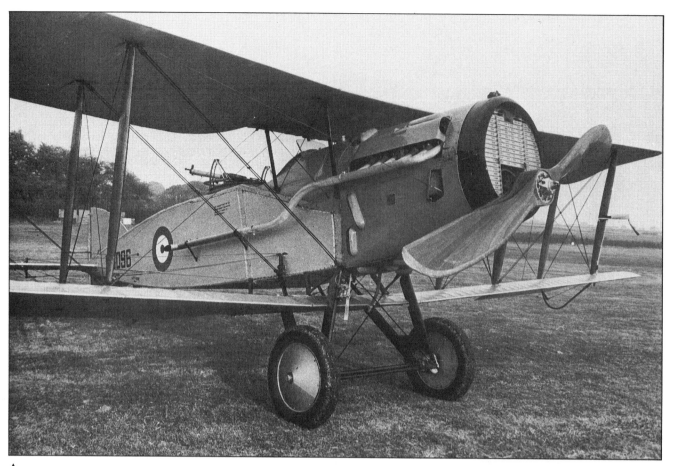

In its aluminium dope finish, with grey cowling and black radiator frame, D8096 looks more attractive than in the PC10 khaki scheme applied from July 1983 at Old Warden. (R Moulton)

DRAWN BY G A G COX

Scrap views
Structure
▼

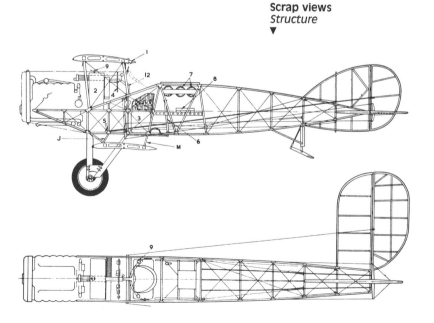

Numerical key
1. Compass. 2, 3. Petrol tanks. 4. Instrument panel. 5. Rudder bar. 6. Gunner's lever. 7. Three machine gun drums. 8. Sliding seat. 9. Filler caps. 10. Switch. 11. Sliding access door. 12. Machine gun mounting.

Key to sketches
1. Inclinometer. 2. Altimeter. 3. Air speed indicator. 4. Engine rpm. 5. Air pressure. 6. Oil pressure. 7. Petrol cock. 8. Water temperature. 9. Compass card. 10. Magneto switch. 11. Navigation/landing lights. 12. Air pressure control to petrol tanks. 13. Watch.

Close-up of cockpits give Scarff mounting detail for the gas-cooled Vickers machine gun and show simple flight controls for the pilot in D8096, the Shuttleworth Collection's machine which is kept at Old Warden and flown regularly each year. (R Moulton) ▶

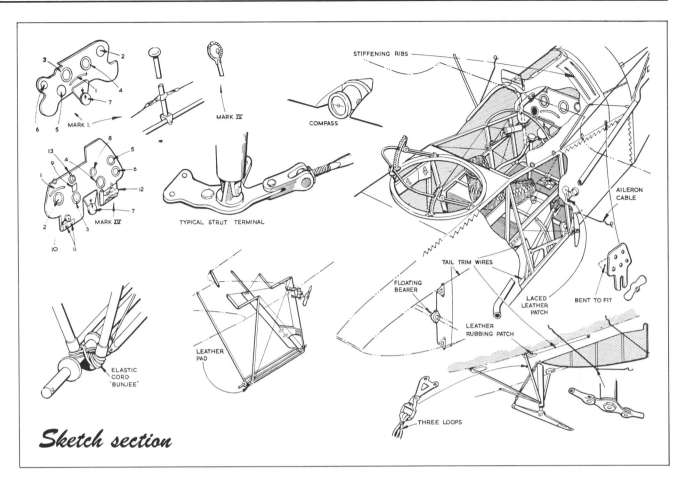

STIFFENING RIBS

MARK IV

COMPASS

MARK I.

AILERON CABLE

MARK IV

TYPICAL STRUT TERMINAL

TAIL TRIM WIRES

FLOATING BEARER

LACED LEATHER PATCH

BENT TO FIT

LEATHER RUBBING PATCH

ELASTIC CORD "BUNJEE"

LEATHER PAD

THREE LOOPS

Sketch section

THIS MACHINE MUST NOT BE FLOWN WITHOUT PASSENGER OR EQUIVALENT WEIGHT IN GUNNERS COCKPIT

De Havilland DH2

Country of origin: Great Britain.
Type: Single-seat fighter.
Powerplant: One Gnome Monosoupape nine-cylinder rotary engine rated at 100hp or Le Rhône rated at 110hp.
Dimensions: Wing span 28ft 3in *8.61m*; length 25ft 2½in *7.68m*; height 9ft 6½in *2.91m*; wing area 249 sq ft *23.13m²*.
Weights: Empty 943lb *428kg*; loaded 1441lb *654kg*.
Performance: (Monosoupape) Maximum speed 93mph *150kph* at ground level; time to 10,000ft *3050m*, 24.75min; service ceiling 14,000ft *4265m*; endurance 2.75hr.
Armament: One fixed or flexibly mounted Lewis machine gun or (some aircraft) two fixed Lewis machine guns.
Service: First flight early 1915; service entry July 1915.

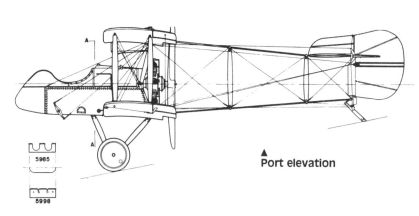

▲
Port elevation

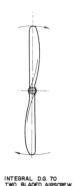

INTEGRAL D.G. 70
TWO BLADED AIRSCREW.

DRAWN BY PETER G COOKSLEY

▲
Propeller

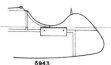

LEFT: VARIOUS TYPES OF AMMUNITION DRUM RACK WERE FITTED. THESE WERE SECURED BY TWO ROUND-HEAD BOLTS WITH WASHERS. NUMBERS INDICATE REPRESENTATIVE SERIALS OF MACHINES THUS FITTED.

Wooden hangars, with curtain fronts, a DH2 on push-back and two others waiting action – a scene that would be typical of 1915–16 when the pusher fighter was a fortunate answer to the Fokker menace. (H Woodman)
▼

Small numbers of DH2s served in the Middle East during 1917. This is from No 14 Sqn in Palestine, which unit formed the nucleus of No 111 Sqn in 1917. (A Imrie)

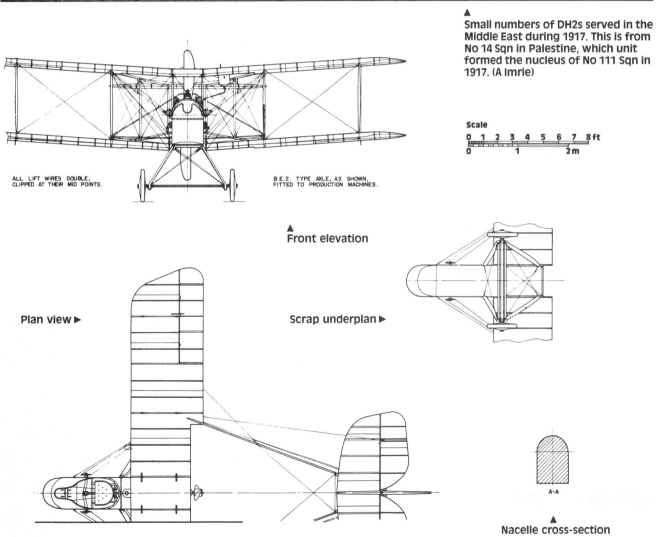

ALL LIFT WIRES DOUBLE, CLIPPED AT THEIR MID POINTS.

B.E.2. TYPE AXLE, AS SHOWN, FITTED TO PRODUCTION MACHINES.

▲
Front elevation

Scale

0 1 2 3 4 5 6 7 8 ft
0 1 2m

Plan view ▶

Scrap underplan ▶

A-A

▲
Nacelle cross-section

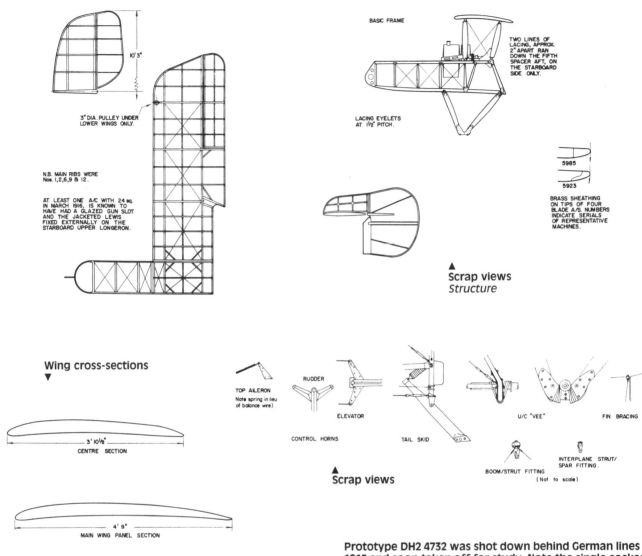

3" DIA. PULLEY UNDER LOWER WINGS ONLY.

N.B. MAIN RIBS WERE Nos. 1, 2, 6, 9 & 12.

AT LEAST ONE A/C WITH 24 sq. IN MARCH 1916, IS KNOWN TO HAVE HAD A GLAZED GUN SLOT AND THE JACKETED LEWIS FIXED EXTERNALLY ON THE STARBOARD UPPER LONGERON.

BASIC FRAME

TWO LINES OF LACING, APPROX. 2" APART RAN DOWN THE FIFTH SPACER AFT, ON THE STARBOARD SIDE ONLY.

LACING EYELETS AT 1½" PITCH.

5985
5923

BRASS SHEATHING ON TIPS OF FOUR BLADE A/S. NUMBERS INDICATE SERIALS OF REPRESENTATIVE MACHINES.

▲ **Scrap views**
Structure

Wing cross-sections
▼

CENTRE SECTION
3' 10½"

MAIN WING PANEL SECTION
4' 9"

TOP AILERON
Note spring in lieu of balance wire)

RUDDER

ELEVATOR

CONTROL HORNS

TAIL SKID

U/C "VEE"

FIN BRACING

BOOM/STRUT FITTING

INTERPLANE STRUT/ SPAR FITTING.
(Not to scale)

▲ **Scrap views**

Prototype DH2 4732 was shot down behind German lines in 1915 and soon taken off for study. Note the single cockade on the wing. (H Woodman)
▼

Scrap views
Markings and seams
▼

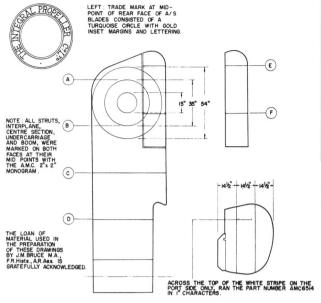

LEFT: TRADE MARK AT MID-POINT OF REAR FACE OF A/S BLADES CONSISTED OF A TURQUOISE CIRCLE WITH GOLD INSET MARGINS AND LETTERING.

THE INTEGRAL PROPELLER C? L?P

15" 35" 54"

NOTE: ALL STRUTS, INTERPLANE, CENTRE SECTION, UNDERCARRIAGE AND BOOM, WERE MARKED ON BOTH FACES AT THEIR MID POINTS WITH THE A.M.C. 2" x 2" MONOGRAM.

14½" 14½" 14½"

THE LOAN OF MATERIAL USED IN THE PREPARATION OF THESE DRAWINGS BY J.M.BRUCE M.A., F.R.Hist s., A.R.Aes. IS GRATEFULLY ACKNOWLEDGED.

ACROSS THE TOP OF THE WHITE STRIPE ON THE PORT SIDE ONLY, RAN THE PART NUMBER AMC65I4 IN I" CHARACTERS.

▲
Apart from operational use by No 14 and No 111 Squadrons, DH2s were used for training by 22 Reserve Squadron at Abu Qir in Egypt in October 1917. The identity of the Middle East DH2 seen here in flight is not known. (A Imrie)

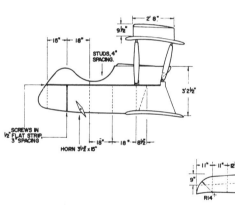

2' 8"
9½"
18" 18"
STUDS, 4" SPACING
3'2½"
SCREWS IN ½" FLAT STRIP, 3" SPACING
HORN 3½" x 15"
18" 18" 8½"

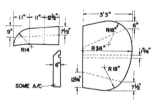

11" 11" 12½"
9"
7½"
R14
6"
SOME A/C

3' 3"
R18"
6"
R30"
I¾"
R 18"
7½"
12¼"

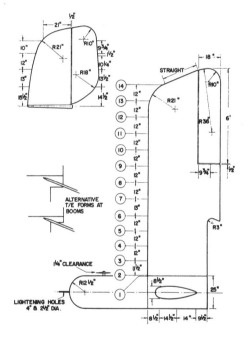

½"
21"
10"
R21"
R10"
9¾"
1½"
12"
R18"
10¼"
13"
13½"
15½"
14½"

STRAIGHT
18"
R10"
R21"
R36
6'
9¾"
½"

14 12"
13 12"
12 12"
11
10
9 12"
8 12"
7 12"
6 13"
5
4
3
2 1½"
1 11½"

ALTERNATIVE T/E FORMS AT BOOMS

1¼" CLEARANCE
R12½"
8½"
25"
R3"
LIGHTENING HOLES 4" & 2½" DIA.
8½" 14½" 14" 9½"

Scale
0 1 2 3 4 5 6 7 8 ft
0 1 2 m

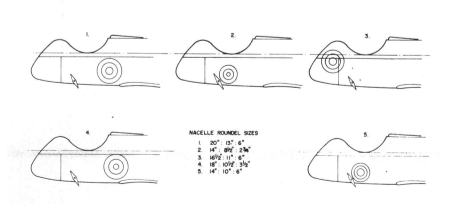

1.
2.
3.
4.
NACELLE ROUNDEL SIZES
1. 20" : 13" : 6"
2. 14" : 8½" : 2¾"
3. 16½" : 11" : 6"
4. 18" : 10½" : 3½"
5. 14" : 10" : 6"

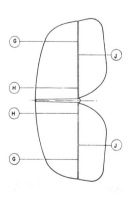
5.

G
J
H
H
J
G

NB. SEAMS IN 36" WIDE FABRIC INDICATED BY LINES A TO J.

Royal Aircraft Factory BE2c

Country of origin: Great Britain.
Type: Two-seat reconnaissance aircraft (flown also as single-seat bomber or night fighter).
Powerplant: One Renault engine rated at 70hp or (later aircraft) RAF 1a eight-cylinder engine rated at 90hp.

Dimensions: Wing span 37ft 0in *11.28m*; length 27ft 3in *8.31m*; height 11ft 1½in *3.39m*; wing area 371 sq ft *34.47m²*.
Weights: Loaded (RAF 1a) 2142lb *971kg*.
Performance: Maximum speed 72mph *116kph* at 6500ft *1980m*; service ceiling 10,000ft *3050m*; endurance 3.25hr.

Armament: One fixed or flexibly mounted Lewis machine gun, plus bombs beneath wings.
Service: First flight summer 1914; service entry April 1915.

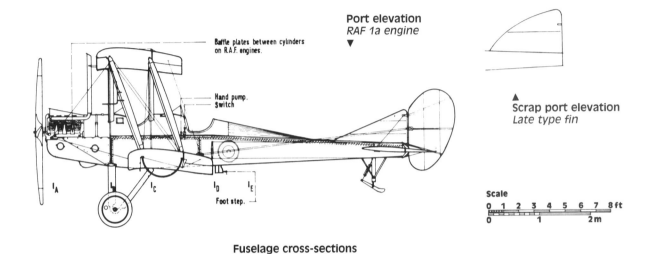

Baffle plates between cylinders on R.A.F. engines.

Hand pump.
Switch

Foot step.

Port elevation
RAF 1a engine
▼

▲
Scrap port elevation
Late type fin

Scale

Fuselage cross-sections
▼

Lewis gun mounting

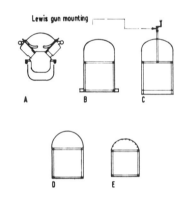

A   B   C

D   E

▲
The cockpit of Leefe Robinson's BE2c 2693, from which he destroyed Zeppelin SL11. (J M Bruce/G S Leslie)

▲
Propeller

Scrap port elevation
Typical armament
▼

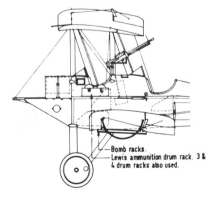

Bomb racks.
Lewis ammunition drum rack. 3 & 4 drum racks also used.

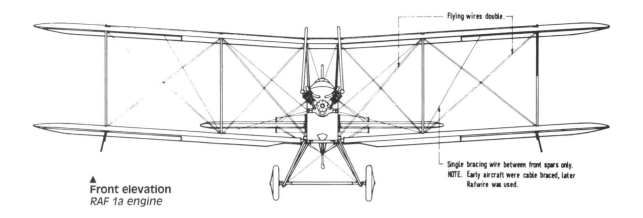

Flying wires double.

Single bracing wire between front spars only.
NOTE. Early aircraft were cable braced, later Rafwire was used.

▲ **Front elevation**
RAF 1a engine

Colour notes
Early BE2cs were covered in linen, clear-doped and varnished. Top decking of fuselage and struts were varnished wood, metal parts being painted grey. From mid-1916 upper surfaces were painted khaki-green (PC10), including ply decking and fuselage sides. Aircraft number usually appeared on fin but varied both in style and size.

DRAWN BY IAN R STAIR

BE2c 1741, built by British and Colonial, as it was at Farnborough on 6 February 1916. The Lewis gun mounting is just one of the many variations used on this aircraft. (RAE Crown Copyright/H Woodman)
▼

▲
**No 4112 of No 39 Home Defence Squadron at Sutton's Farm,
Hornchurch. 2nd Lt Frederick Sowrey shot down Zeppelin
L32 whilst flying this machine on 24 September 1916.
(H Woodman)**

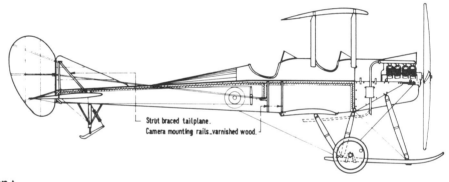

Strut braced tailplane.
Camera mounting rails_varnished wood.

Starboard elevation▲
*Renault engine and skid undercarriage.
Alternative exhausts shown dotted
(vertical exhausts also fitted).*

Scrap underplan
▼

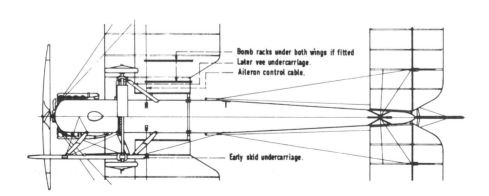

Bomb racks under both wings if fitted
Later vee undercarriage.
Aileron control cable.

Early skid undercarriage.

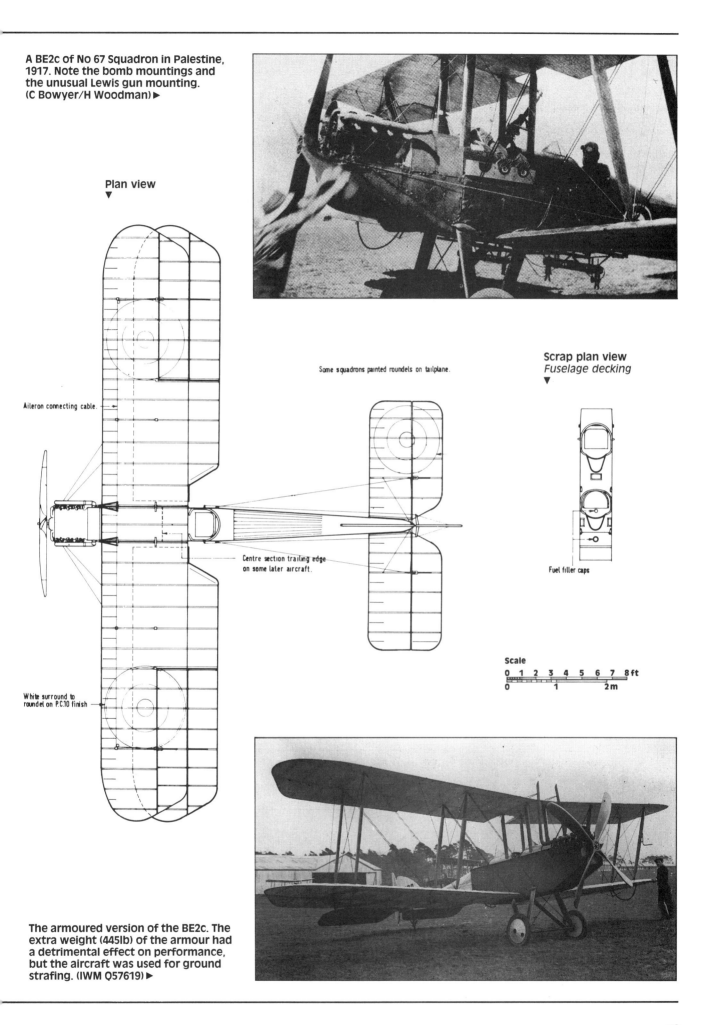

A BE2c of No 67 Squadron in Palestine, 1917. Note the bomb mountings and the unusual Lewis gun mounting. (C Bowyer/H Woodman) ▶

Plan view
▼

Aileron connecting cable.

White surround to roundel on P.C.10 finish

Some squadrons painted roundels on tailplane.

Centre section trailing edge on some later aircraft.

Scrap plan view
Fuselage decking
▼

Fuel filler caps

Scale

0 1 2 3 4 5 6 7 8 ft

0   1   2 m

The armoured version of the BE2c. The extra weight (445lb) of the armour had a detrimental effect on performance, but the aircraft was used for ground strafing. (IWM Q57619) ▶

Royal Aircraft Factory FE2b

Country of origin: Great Britain.
Type: Two-seat fighter and patrol aircraft.
Powerplant: One Beardmore engine rated at 120hp.
Dimensions: Wing span 47ft 9in *14.55m*; length 32ft 3in *9.83m*; height 12ft 7½in *3.85m*.
Weights: Empty 1993lb *904kg*; loaded 2967lb *1346kg*.
Performance: Maximum speed 81mph *130.5kph* at 6500ft *1980m*; time to 6500ft, 18.9min; service ceiling 11,000ft *3350m*; endurance 3.5hr.
Armament: One (later two) flexibly mounted Lewis machine guns.
Service: First flight March 1915; service entry May 1915.

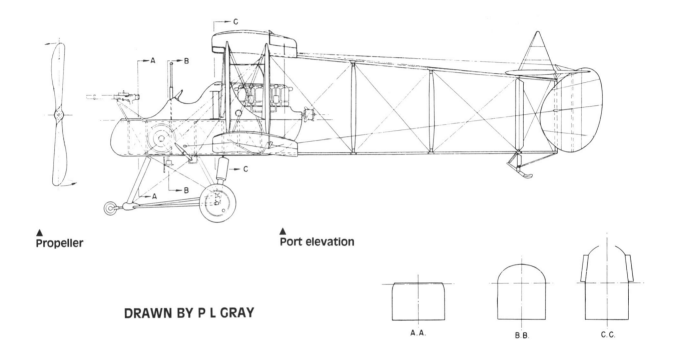

▲ Propeller

▲ Port elevation

DRAWN BY P L GRAY

A.A.   B.B.   C.C.

▲ Fuselage cross-sections

The frailty of the FE2b and exposure of the crew in their shallow-sided cockpits is evident in this view of one from the first production batch. (IWM Q60549)
▼

▲
Prototype FE2d, fitted with a 250hp Rolls-Royce Eagle engine, with stack-type exhausts. On production aircraft the engine installation was much tidier. (IWM Q56630)

Plan view ▶

Wing cross-section
▼

D.D.

D   D

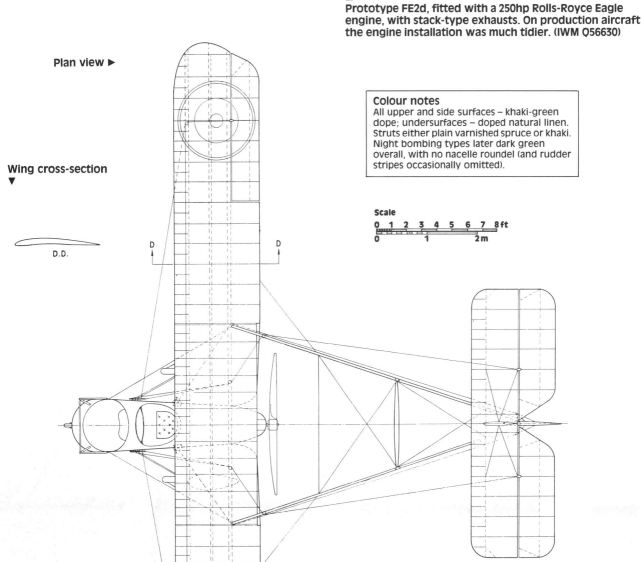

Colour notes
All upper and side surfaces – khaki-green dope; undersurfaces – doped natural linen. Struts either plain varnished spruce or khaki. Night bombing types later dark green overall, with no nacelle roundel (and rudder stripes occasionally omitted).

Scale
0 1 2 3 4 5 6 7 8 ft
0   1   2 m

▲
Forward guns on pusher aircraft avoided the problems of
synchronisation, but an FE2b chasing a manoeuvrable
single-seater was said by Oliver Stewart to be 'comical'.
(IWM Q27644)

An early FE2b with nosewheel undercarriage to prevent
overturning, and having a bracket for the single Lewis gun
in front of the observer. (IWM 67543)
▼

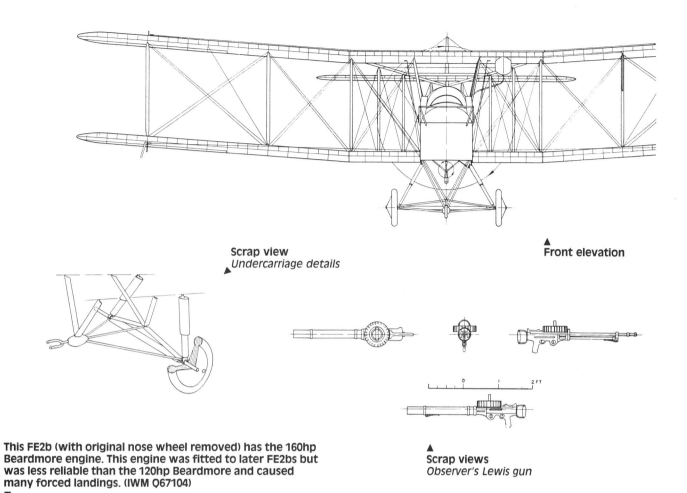

Scrap view
Undercarriage details

▲
Front elevation

▲
Scrap views
Observer's Lewis gun

This FE2b (with original nose wheel removed) has the 160hp Beardmore engine. This engine was fitted to later FE2bs but was less reliable than the 120hp Beardmore and caused many forced landings. (IWM Q67104)
▼

Royal Aircraft Factory SE5 and SE5a

Country of origin: Great Britain.
Type: Single-seat scout.
Powerplant: One Hispano-Suiza engine rated at 150hp, (SE5a) Hispano-Suiza rated at 200hp or 220hp or Wolseley Viper rated at 200hp.
Dimensions: Wing span 26ft 7½in *8.12m*; length 21ft 4in *6.50m*, (SE5a) 20ft 11in *6.38m*; height 9ft 6in *2.90m*.
Weights: Empty 1399lb *634kg*, (SE5a) 1400lb *635kg*; loaded 1930lb *875kg*, (SE5a) 1953lb *886kg*.
Performance: Maximum speed 98mph *158kph* at 15,000ft *4570m*, (SE5a) 121mph *195kph* at 15,000ft; time to 15,000ft, 29.5min, (SE5a, 200hp Hispano) 18.8min.
Armament: One fixed Vickers machine gun and one fixed Lewis machine gun.
Service: First flight (prototype SE5) December 1916; service entry (SE5) March 1917, (SE5a) mid-1917.

DRAWN BY G A G COX

Fuselage cross-sections

Propeller details
▼

FOUR-BLADE AIRSCREW ON
B 4863

EXTERNAL GRAVITY TANK ON EARLY S.E.5

Port elevation, SE5
▼

B 4863 WAS FLOWN BY
MAJOR J. B. MC.CUDDEN V.C.

THIS WIRE NOT STANDARD

E 4863

G

WHITE

A   B   C   D   E

SE5a B4885, which came down in Holland on 6 January 1918. This picture shows it in Dutch service as SE 214; the British roundels have been overpainted with the orange disc of the Netherlands. (Luchtvaartafdeeling/ H Woodman)
▼

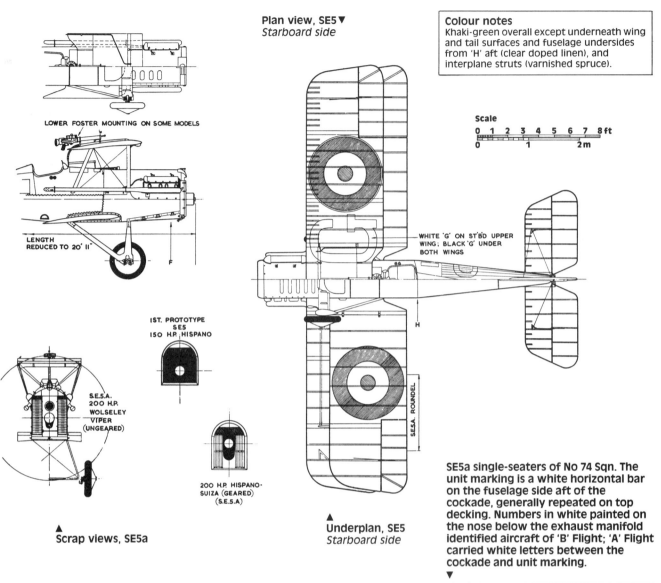

LOWER FOSTER MOUNTING ON SOME MODELS

LENGTH
REDUCED TO 20' 11"

F

S.E.5.A.
200 H.P.
WOLSELEY
VIPER
(UNGEARED)

1ST. PROTOTYPE
SE5
150 H.P. HISPANO

200 H.P. HISPANO-
SUIZA (GEARED)
(S.E.5.A)

Plan view, SE5 ▼
Starboard side

WHITE 'G' ON ST'B'D UPPER
WING; BLACK 'G' UNDER
BOTH WINGS

S.E.5A. ROUNDEL

Scale

0 1 2 3 4 5 6 7 8 ft
0   1   2 m

▲
Scrap views, SE5a

▲
Underplan, SE5
Starboard side

SE5a single-seaters of No 74 Sqn. The
unit marking is a white horizontal bar
on the fuselage side aft of the
cockade, generally repeated on top
decking. Numbers in white painted on
the nose below the exhaust manifold
identified aircraft of 'B' Flight; 'A' Flight
carried white letters between the
cockade and unit marking.
▼

▲
Possibly a training machine – note the large rudder streamer and box fairing on lower fuselage side ahead of cockpit to catch cartridges. This SE5a was Martinsyde-built. (A Imrie)

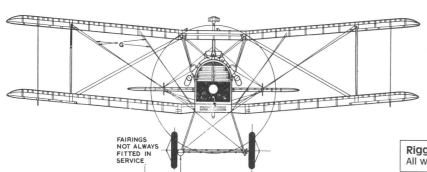

G

FAIRINGS
NOT ALWAYS
FITTED IN
SERVICE

Rigging notes
All wires streamlined. Wires 'G' doubled.

▲
Front elevation, SE5

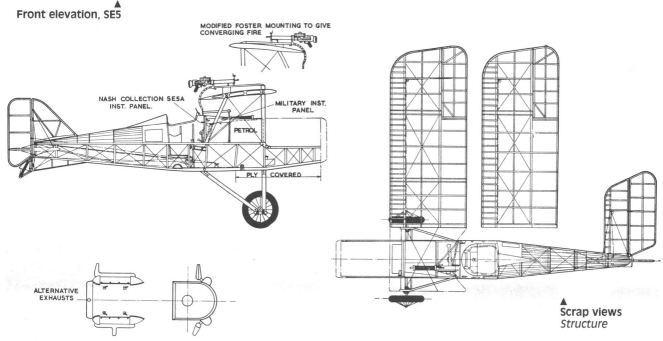

MODIFIED FOSTER MOUNTING TO GIVE
CONVERGING FIRE

NASH COLLECTION SE5A
INST. PANEL.

MILITARY INST.
PANEL

PETROL

PLY   COVERED

ALTERNATIVE
EXHAUSTS

▲
Scrap views
Structure

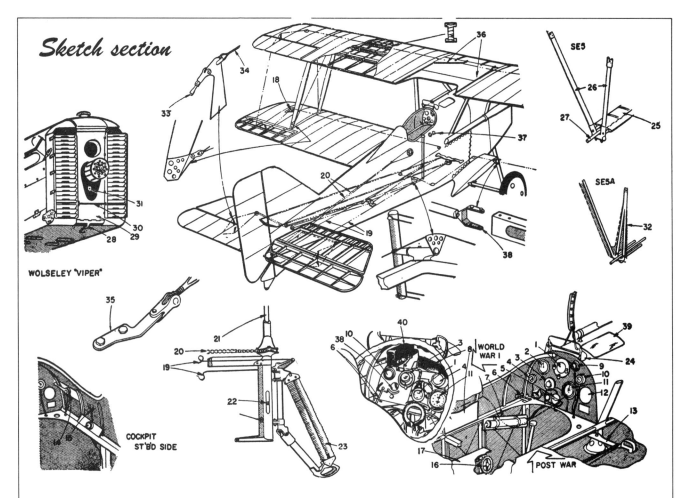

Sketch section

SE5

SE5A

WOLSELEY 'VIPER'

COCKPIT ST'B'D SIDE

WORLD WAR I

POST WAR

Key to sketches

1. Compass mounting. 2. Altimeter. 3. Petrol switch. 4. Oil pressure. 5. Petrol switch. 6. Throttle and compensator. 7. Priming pump. 8. Map pocket. 9. Water pump. 10. Air pressure gauge. 11. Air speed indicator. 12. Instrument position blanked off. 13. Aluminium rudder bar. 14. Radiator shutter control. 15. Four leads out to switches 37. 16. Tail trim wheel. 17. Ply seat platform. 18. Pulley inspection window (also under top wing and on tailplane). 19. Skid steering wires. 20. Tail trim chain raises or lowers through worm gear the tube 21 at each end of which are tail bracing attachments 22. 23. Telescopic tubes inside springs prevent buckling. 24. Metal fairings to windscreen pivots. 25. Door hinged at front edge. 26. Streamlined steel tubes. 27. Axle held down by bungee. 28. Radiator drain. 29. Flat metal panel. 30. Shutter operating rod. 31. Interrupter gear oil pump and drive. 32. Circular steel tube faired with wood. 33. Streamlined wire to elevator. 34. Stranded wire to joystick. 35. Tail bracing wire terminal. 36. Petrol expansion pipes. 37. Spar attachment. 38. Radiator temperature. 39. Window. 40. Vickers gun.

◀ Random positions of instruments and engine controls in the SE5 were typical of the period. To illuminate the dials, a pair of mica windows were let into the upper fuselage, but these soon became obscure with exposure to sunlight. (J M Bruce/G S Leslie)

Sopwith Buffalo

Country of origin: Great Britain.
Type: Two-seat armoured contact patrol aircraft.
Powerplant: One Bentley BR2 rotary engine rated at 230hp.
Dimensions: Wing span 34ft 6in *10.52m*;

length 23ft 3½in *7.10m*; height 9ft 6in *2.90m*; wing area 340 sq ft *31.59m²*.
Weights: Empty 2175lb *986kg*; loaded 3071lb *1393kg*.
Performance: Maximum speed 114mph *184.5kph* at 1000ft *305m*; time to 3000ft

915m, 5min; service ceiling 9000ft *2750m*.
Armament: One fixed Vickers machine gun and one flexibly mounted Lewis machine gun.
Service: First flight autumn 1918.

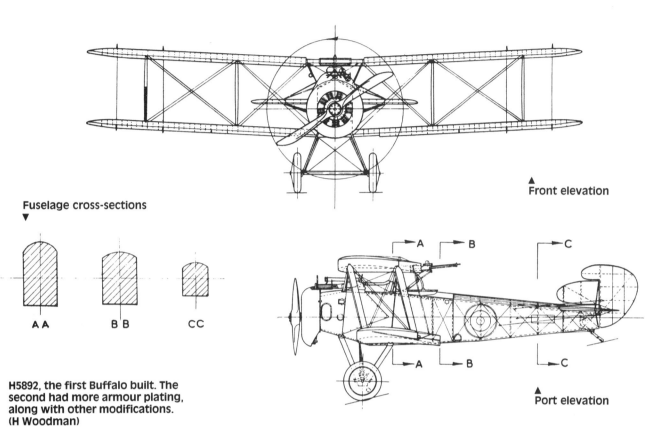

▲ Front elevation

Fuselage cross-sections
▼

A A   B B   C C

▲ Port elevation

H5892, the first Buffalo built. The second had more armour plating, along with other modifications. (H Woodman)

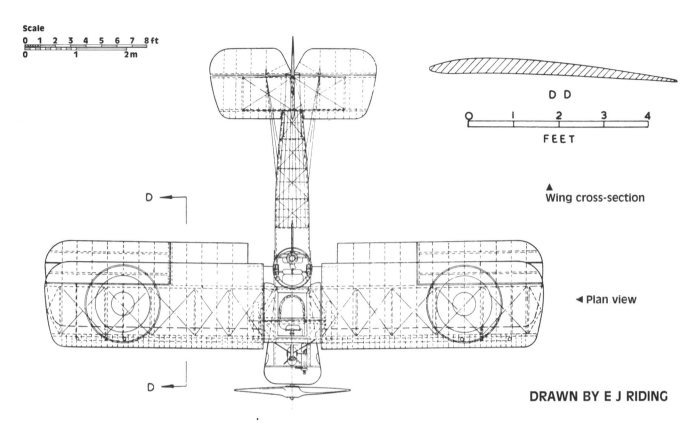

0 1 2 3 4 5 6 7 8 ft

0   1   2 m

D D

0   1   2   3   4

FEET

▲ Wing cross-section

◀ Plan view

D →

D →

DRAWN BY E J RIDING

This photograph of the second Buffalo, H5893, provides a comparison with H5892. Note the revised flank fairings on the engine cowling, the extended fuselage armour and the enlarged rudder with modified horn balance. H5893 had a Scarff ring on the rear cockpit from the outset. (J M Bruce)

▲
The second Buffalo, H5893, at Martlesham Heath, where it had arrived for trials on 18 November 1918. With H5892 it was allotted to the RAF in Europe on 29 April 1919, but was still at Martlesham on 10 May when it crashed on a landing approach. (J M Bruce)

▼

Sopwith F1 Camel

Country of origin: Great Britain.
Type: Single-seat scout.
Powerplant: One Clerget engine rated at 110hp or 130hp, Le Rhône rated at 110hp or Bentley BRI rated at 150hp.
Dimensions: Wing span 28ft 0in *8.53m*;

length 18ft 9in *5.72m*; height 8ft 6in *2.59m*.
Weights: Empty 929lb *421kg*; loaded 1453lb *659kg*.
Performance: (130hp Clerget) Maximum speed 115mph *185kph* at 6500ft *1980m*;

time to 6500ft, 6min; service ceiling 19,000ft *5485m*; endurance 2.5hr.
Armament: Two fixed Vickers machine guns, plus up to four 25lb *11.3kg* bombs.
Service: First flight December 1916; service entry summer 1917.

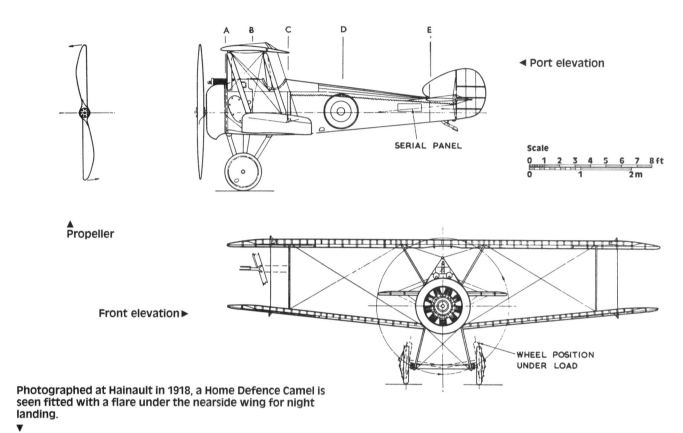

◄ Port elevation

SERIAL PANEL

Scale

▲ Propeller

Front elevation ►

WHEEL POSITION UNDER LOAD

Photographed at Hainault in 1918, a Home Defence Camel is seen fitted with a flare under the nearside wing for night landing.
▼

B 9175

5

▲
Camel 2F1 with 150hp BRI engine, armed with a single offset Vickers gun on the fuselage and an extra Lewis on a special reloading mount above the centre section (IWM)

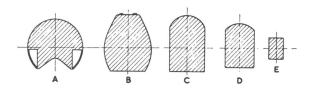

▲
Fuselage cross-sections

DRAWN BY P L GRAY

Night fighter Camel of 44 Sqn with cockpit moved rearwards and twin Foster gun mount above the wing, to avoid flash and permit upward firing as well as re-loading. (J M Bruce/ G S Leslie)
▼

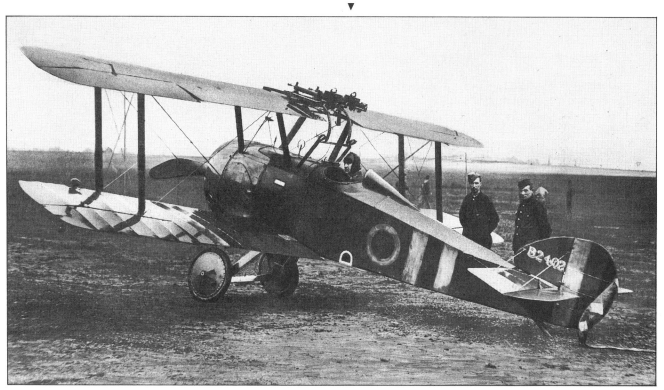

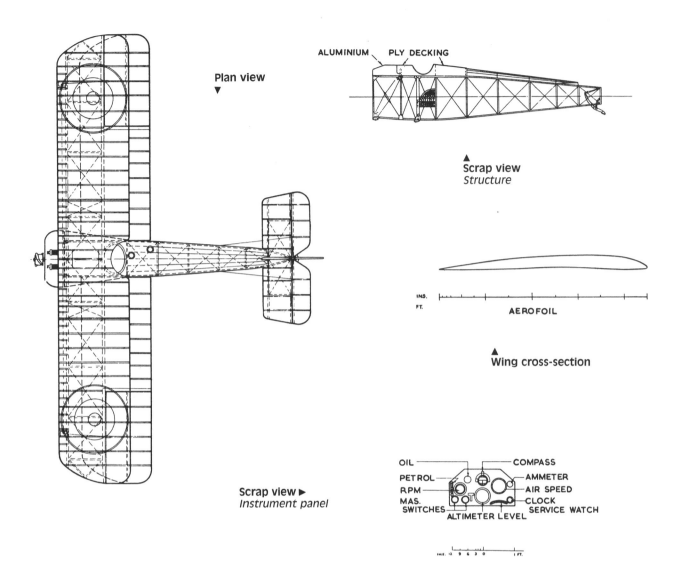

Plan view ▼

ALUMINIUM   PLY DECKING

▲ **Scrap view**
Structure

INS.
FT.
AEROFOIL

▲ **Wing cross-section**

OIL ——————— COMPASS
PETROL ————— AMMETER
RPM ——————— AIR SPEED
MAS. ——————— CLOCK
SWITCHES ————— SERVICE WATCH
ALTIMETER LEVEL

INS. 12 9 6 3 0   1 FT.

Scrap view ▶
Instrument panel

Scrap starboard elevation
▼

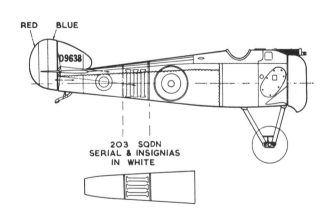

RED   BLUE

O9638

203 SQDN
SERIAL & INSIGNIAS
IN WHITE

Colour notes

Ex-works: Khaki-green dope on upper and side surfaces, clear doped linen underneath, with protective varnish. Roundels against khaki background were thinly outlined in white. Metal and ply panelling usually painted grey, but not invariably so, and metal areas sometimes left bright. Serial number application varied: black on white rectangle on rear fuselage; in same position in plain white; on rudder in black; or on fin in white.

10 Sqn RNAS: 'A' Flight – black and white stripes; 'B' Flight – blue and white stripes; 'C' Flight – red and white stripes. Serial number – white. Stripes fore and aft of roundel, and individual letter – white.

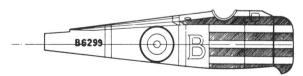

B6299   B

◀ **Scrap starboard elevation**
No 10 Sqn RNAS aircraft

Maurice Farman Shorthorn

Country of origin: France.
Type: Two-seat training and reconnaissance aircraft.
Powerplant: One Renault engine rated at 75hp.

Dimensions: Wing span 53ft 0in *16.15m*; length 30ft 8in *9.35m*; height 10ft 4in *3.15m*; wing area 561 sq ft *52.12m²*.
Weights: Empty 1441lb *654kg*; loaded 2046lb *928kg*.

Performance: Maximum speed 66mph *106kph* at sea level; time to 3000ft *915m*, 15min; endurance 3.75hr.
Armament: None.
Service: Service entry summer 1913.

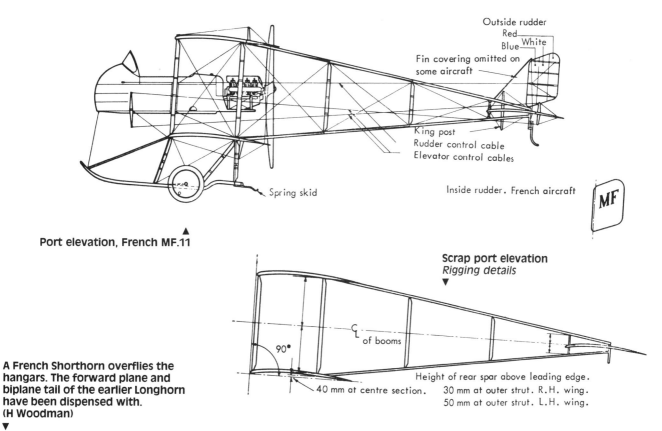

Port elevation, French MF.11

Scrap port elevation
Rigging details

A French Shorthorn overflies the hangars. The forward plane and biplane tail of the earlier Longhorn have been dispensed with. (H Woodman)

◄ Captured Farman 'in the rough' but little damaged, and the subject of German curiosity. (A Imrie)

Scale

0 1 2 3 4 5 6 7 8 ft

0   1   2m

French Roundel
— Blue
— White
— Red

DRAWN BY IAN R STAIR

Scrap underplan
▼

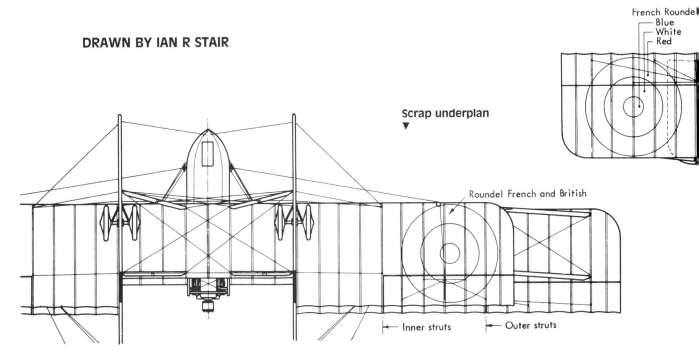

Roundel French and British

|← Inner struts →| |← Outer struts →|

Rigging of centre section

5 mm To small to show at this scale

Aileron connecting cable

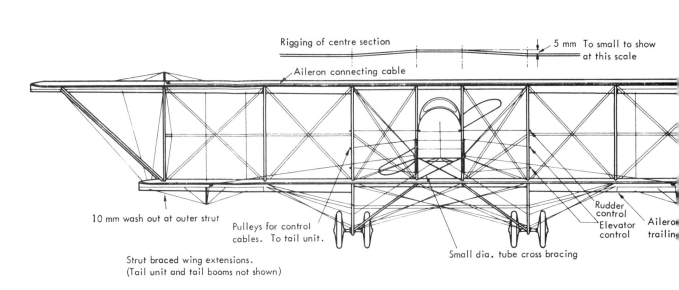

10 mm wash out at outer strut

Pulleys for control cables. To tail unit.

Strut braced wing extensions.
(Tail unit and tail booms not shown)

Small dia. tube cross bracing

Rudder control

Elevator control

Aileron trailing

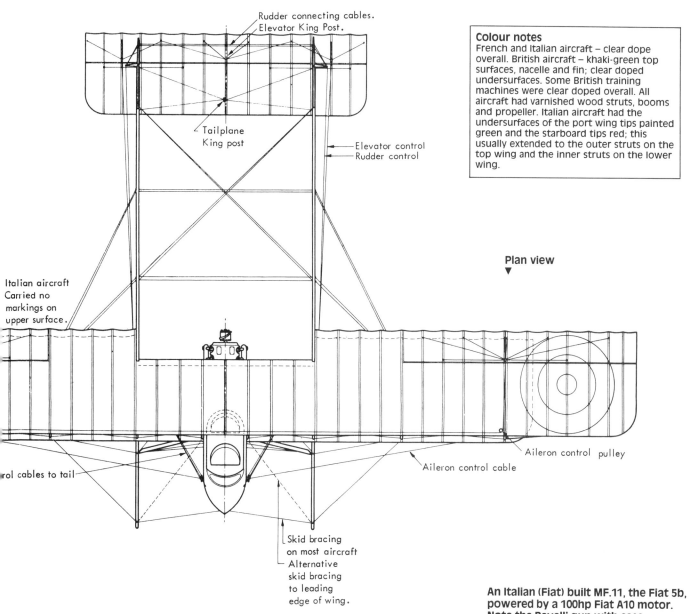

Rudder connecting cables.
Elevator King Post.

Tailplane
King post

Elevator control
Rudder control

Colour notes
French and Italian aircraft – clear dope overall. British aircraft – khaki-green top surfaces, nacelle and fin; clear doped undersurfaces. Some British training machines were clear doped overall. All aircraft had varnished wood struts, booms and propeller. Italian aircraft had the undersurfaces of the port wing tips painted green and the starboard tips red; this usually extended to the outer struts on the top wing and the inner struts on the lower wing.

Plan view
▼

Italian aircraft
Carried no
markings on
upper surface.

Aileron control pulley

...rol cables to tail

Aileron control cable

Skid bracing
on most aircraft
Alternative
skid bracing
to leading
edge of wing.

Front elevation
▼

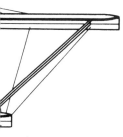

...m wash in at outer strut.
...h 15 mm droop at

An Italian (Fiat) built MF.11, the Fiat 5b, powered by a 100hp Fiat A10 motor. Note the Revelli gun with case collector box fitted. (Ufficio Documentazione/H Woodman)
▼

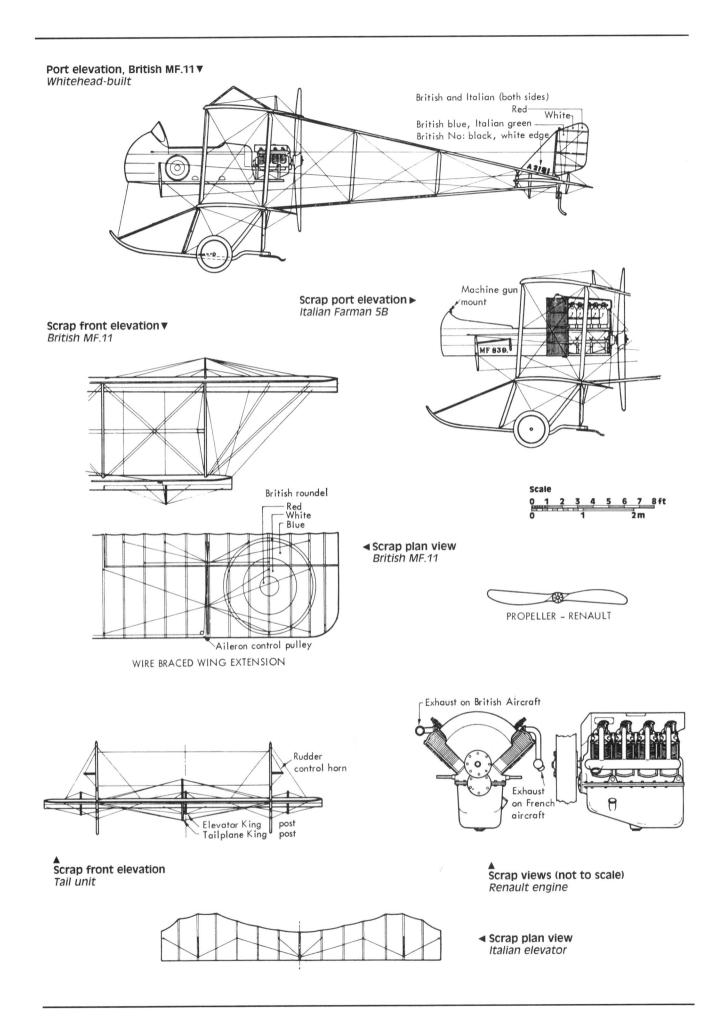

Port elevation, British MF.11 ▼
Whitehead-built

British and Italian (both sides)
Red — White
British blue, Italian green
British No: black, white edge

A2191

Scrap port elevation ▶
Italian Farman 5B

Machine gun mount

MF 839.

Scrap front elevation ▼
British MF.11

British roundel
Red
White
Blue

◄ Scrap plan view
British MF.11

Scale
0 1 2 3 4 5 6 7 8 ft
0 1 2 m

PROPELLER – RENAULT

Aileron control pulley

WIRE BRACED WING EXTENSION

Rudder control horn

Elevator King post
Tailplane King post

▲
Scrap front elevation
Tail unit

Exhaust on British Aircraft

Exhaust on French aircraft

▲
Scrap views (not to scale)
Renault engine

◄ Scrap plan view
Italian elevator

Morane Saulnier Type L

Country of origin: France.
Type: Single-seat scout.
Powerplant: One Gnome or Le Rhône engine rated at 80hp.
Dimensions: (Prototype) Wing span 34ft

0in *10.36m*; length 20ft 9in *6.32m*; wing area 172 sq ft *16.0m²*.
Weights: Loaded 839lb *380kg*.
Performance: (Gnome) Maximum speed 76mph *122kph*; initial climb rate 345ft/

min *105m/min*.
Armament: None, although later various *ad hoc* ordnance (eg bombs) was carried.
Service: First flight 1913.

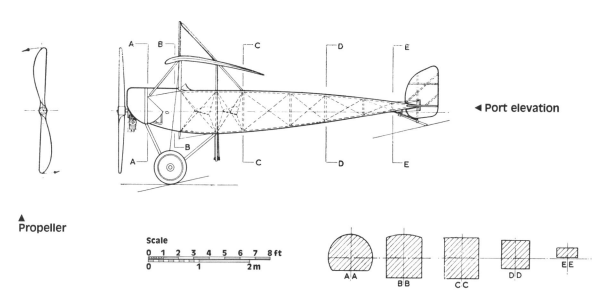

▲ Propeller

◄ Port elevation

Scale
0 1 2 3 4 5 6 7 8ft
0   1   2m

A A   B B   C C   D D   E E

▲ Fuselage cross-sections

A Morane L of No 1 Wing RNAS at Imbros, 1915. Moranes in British service had modifications to the undercarriage, rudder and elevator, and were fitted with 80hp Le Rhône engines. (H Woodman)
▼

▲
The classic 'Parasol', an important workhorse during the early years of the war. (H Woodman)

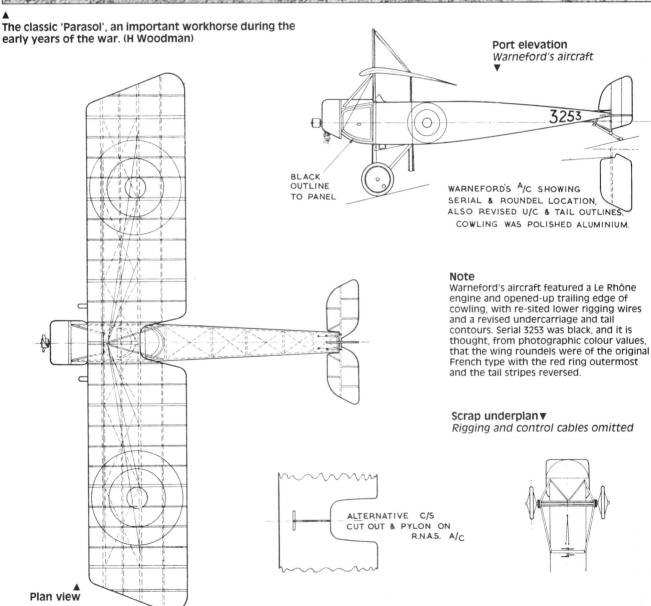

BLACK
OUTLINE
TO PANEL

Port elevation
Warneford's aircraft
▼

3253

WARNEFORD'S A/C SHOWING
SERIAL & ROUNDEL LOCATION,
ALSO REVISED U/C & TAIL OUTLINES.
COWLING WAS POLISHED ALUMINIUM.

Note
Warneford's aircraft featured a Le Rhône
engine and opened-up trailing edge of
cowling, with re-sited lower rigging wires
and a revised undercarriage and tail
contours. Serial 3253 was black, and it is
thought, from photographic colour values,
that the wing roundels were of the original
French type with the red ring outermost
and the tail stripes reversed.

Scrap underplan▼
Rigging and control cables omitted

ALTERNATIVE C/S
CUT OUT & PYLON ON
R.N.A.S. A/C

▲
Plan view

DRAWN BY P L GRAY

▲
A Red Air Fleet trainer on which, following the French practice, fabric has been stripped from the wings, allowing the aeroplane only to 'ground hop'. (H Woodman)

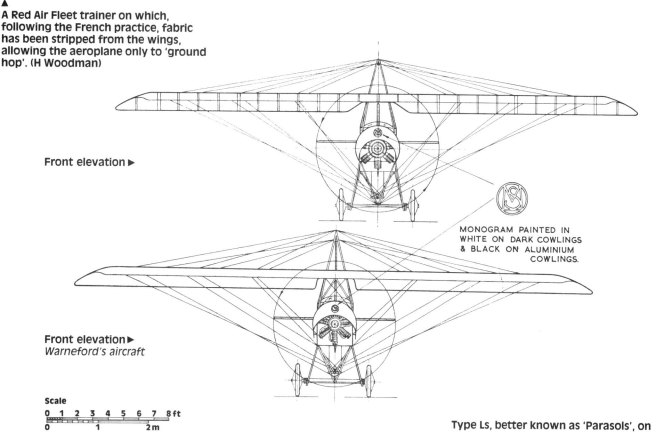

Front elevation ▶

MONOGRAM PAINTED IN WHITE ON DARK COWLINGS & BLACK ON ALUMINIUM COWLINGS.

Front elevation ▶
Warneford's aircraft

Scale
0 1 2 3 4 5 6 7 8 ft
0   1   2 m

Type Ls, better known as 'Parasols', on the Morane Saulnier airfield at Villacoublay in 1915. (H Woodman)
▼

Nieuport 11

Country of origin: France.
Type: Single-seat fighter.
Powerplant: One Le Rhône engine rated at 80hp.
Dimensions: Wing span 24ft 9¼in

7.55m; length 19ft 0½in 5.80m; height 8ft 0½in 2.45m.
Weights: Take-off 1058lb 480kg.
Performance: Maximum speed 97mph 156kph at sea level; service ceiling

15,100ft 4600m; endurance 2.5hr.
Armament: One fixed Lewis machine gun, plus up to eight Le Prieur rockets.
Service: Service entry 1915.

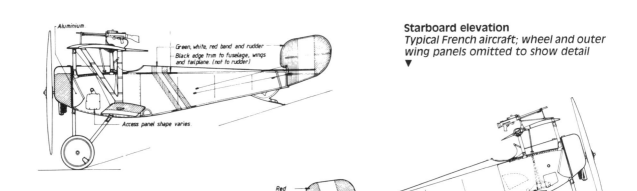

Starboard elevation
Typical French aircraft; wheel and outer wing panels omitted to show detail
▼

▲
Port elevation

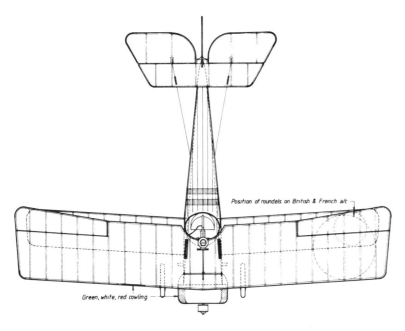

▲
Plan view

DRAWN BY IAN R STAIR

Colour notes
Most Nie 11s were clear-doped overall, but some later aircraft were dark green or camouflaged on the upper surfaces. Italian Nie 11s rarely carried roundels on the top sides of the wings but often on the fuselage; French and British aircraft had roundels on both surfaces of the top wing and on the underside of the lower wing, while British machines had fuselage roundels also.

Notes
Main drawings depict Italian, Macchi-built aircraft, which differed from French Nieuports only in minor details and dimensions.

▲
A French Nieuport 11 in 1916, with the Le Prieur balloon-busting rockets on its interplane struts. The sesquiplane arrangement called for roundels under all wings. (H Woodman)

Nieuport II N1135 of *Escadrille N26* in German hands, 1916. It has a typical shaded, two-tone camouflage scheme with outline edging. (A Imrie)
▼

◄ Gun mountings on the Nieuport 11 enabled re-loading and inclined firing.

Fuselage cross-sections
▼

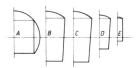

Scrap plan view
Alternative gun mounting
▼

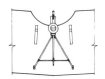

Rear view mirror

Underside of wings green.

Underside of wings red.

▲
Front elevation

Scale
0 1 2 3 4 5 6 7 8 ft
0 1 2 m

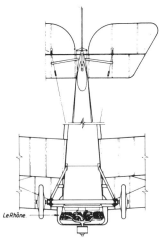

80 h.p. Le Rhône.

Scrap underplan ►

A Nieuport 11 of *Escadrille 26* being inspected by its German captors in July 1916. (K M Molson/H Woodman)
▼

Nieuport 24 and 27

Country of origin: France.
Type: Single-seat fighter.
Powerplant: One Le Rhône engine rated at 120hp.
Dimensions: Wing span 26ft 11in *8.20m*;
length 19ft 2½in *5.85m*; height 7ft 11¼in *2.42m*.
Weights: Take-off 1290lb *585kg*.
Performance: Maximum speed 115.5mph *186kph* at sea level; service
ceiling 18,050ft *5500m*; endurance about 1.5hr.
Armament: One fixed machine gun.
Service: Service entry 1917.

Notes
Nieuport 24bis similar to 24 except for tail unit and ailerons. Nieuport 27 similar except for windscreen, length of used belt chute and split-axle undercarriage. Cowling and cowling panels similar on all three types; Lewis gun could be mounted over top wing.

Port elevation, Nieuport 24

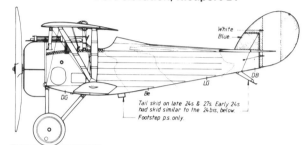

Tail skid on late 24s & 27s. Early 24s had skid similar to the 24bis, below.
Footstep p.s. only.

Scale

0 1 2 3 4 5 6 7 8ft
0 1 2m

DRAWN BY IAN R STAIR

TOP
BOTTOM

▲ Wing cross-sections

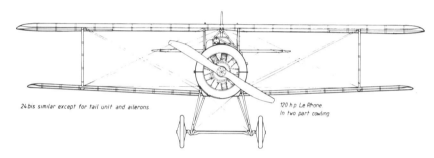

24bis similar except for tail unit and ailerons.

120 h.p. Le Rhone in two part cowling

▲ Front elevation, Nieuport 24

Type 24, serial no N5449, of *Escadrille N89* in German hands after being brought down by *Jagdstaffel 31* with obvious landing gear damage – hence the odd wheels. (A Imrie)
▼

▲
**The forward gun on the Nieuport 23 –
also the 24 – was a neat
installation. (J M Bruce/G S Leslie)**

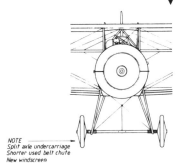

NOTE
*Split axle undercarriage
Shorter used belt chute
New windscreen*

Scrap plan view, Nieuport 24bis
▼

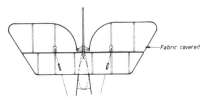

Fabric covered

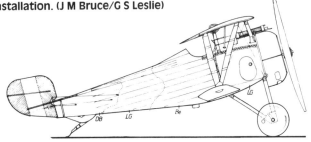

▲
Starboard elevation, Nieuport 24bis

Veneer covered (2 layers)

*Cowling & cowling panels
were similar on all 3
types.
Lewis gun could be
mounted over the top
wing.*

Scale

0 1 2 3 4 5 6 7 8 ft
0   1   2 m

Plan view, Nieuport 24 and 27
▼

Aileron shape NIEUPORT 24 bis

Red White Blue

*Plywood covered leading edge,
top surface only.*

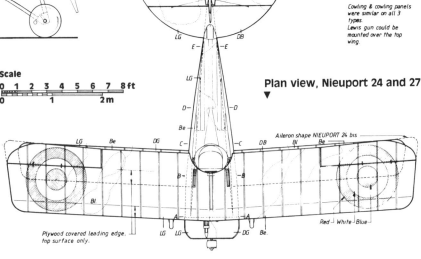

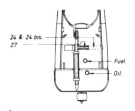

24 & 24 bis.
27

*Fuel.
Oil.*

▲
Scrap plan view, Nieuport 27

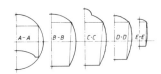

A-A B-B C-C D-D E-E

▲
Fuselage cross-sections

Colour notes
French five-colour camouflage scheme: **Be** –
Beige; **Bl** – Black; **DB** – Dark brown; **DG** – Dark
green; **LG** – Light green. Undersides – clear
doped.

**Captured when with No 29 Sqn in April
1918, this Nieuport 24 was flown by
Lt A G Wingate Gray, who became a
POW. (J M Bruce/G S Leslie)** ▶

SPAD VII

Country of origin: France.
Type: Single-seat scout.
Powerplant: One Hispano-Suiza 8A engine rated at 140hp, 8Aa rated at 175hp or 8Ab rated at 205hp.
Dimensions: Wing span 25ft 8in *7.82m*; length 20ft 3in *6.17m*; height 7ft 0in 2.13m; wing area 192 sq ft *17.84m²*, (1917 model) 195 sq ft *18.12m²*.
Weights: Empty 1177lb *534kg*; loaded 1632lb *740kg*.
Performance: Maximum speed 119mph *192kph* at 6500ft *1980m*, (Hispano 8Aa/8Ab) 132mph *212.5kph*; initial climb rate 810ft/min *247m/min*; service ceiling 17,500ft *5335m*; endurance 2.5hr.
Armament: One fixed Vickers machine gun.
Service: First flight July 1916.

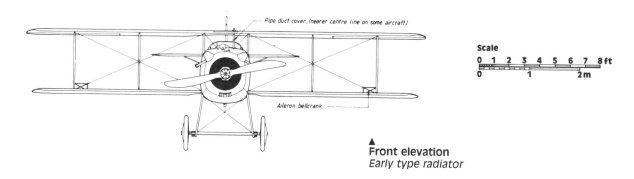

Pipe duct cover, (nearer centre line on some aircraft)

Aileron bellcrank.

▲ **Front elevation**
Early type radiator

Scale

Final arrangement of radiator shutters (open).

◀ **Scrap front elevation**
Late type radiator

Scrap view
Aileron bellcrank
▼

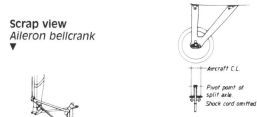

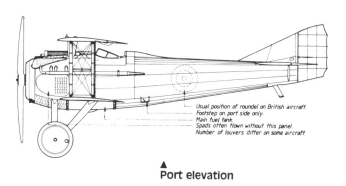

Aircraft C.L.
Pivot point of split axle.
Shock cord omitted.

Scrap views ▲
Undercarriage details

Usual position of roundel on British aircraft.
Footstep on port side only.
Main fuel tank.
Spads often flown without this panel.
Number of louvers differ on some aircraft.

▲
Port elevation

Captain Eddie Rickenbacker's markings on this VII represent the 94th Aero Squadron of the American Expeditionary Force, otherwise known as the 'Escadrille Lafayette'. Top US ace, Rickenbacker went on to a successful career with the Indianapolis Speedway, General Motors and Eastern Airlines, but his SPAD was in fact a XIII.
▼

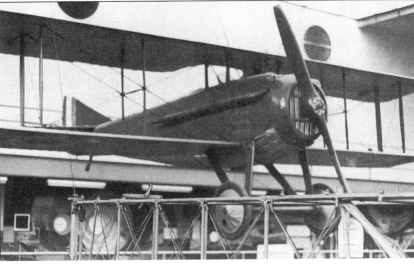

Scale

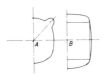

▲
Scrap plan view
Top wing omitted for detail

▲ The SPAD VII was designed by Louis Bechereau around the 150hp Hispano-Suiza and a compact cockpit. Widely respected, it is well preserved in museums around the world; this one is in Prague. (R Moulton)

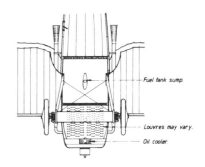

Fuel tank sump.

Louvres may vary.

Oil cooler.

▲
Scrap underplan

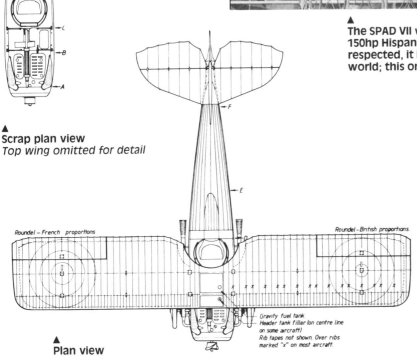

Roundel – French proportions.

Roundel – British proportions.

Gravity fuel tank.
Header tank filler (on centre line on some aircraft)
Rib tapes not shown. Over ribs marked "x" on most aircraft.

▲
Plan view

Carrying Baracca's rampant horse insignia, this SPAD VII is kept in the French Musée de l'Air, though here in a special display at Orly. (R Moulton)
▼

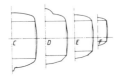

▲
Fuselage cross-sections

DRAWN BY IAN R STAIR

Hanriot HD1

Country of origin: Belgium.
Type: Single-seat scout.
Powerplant: One Le Rhône rotary engine rated at 110hp.
Dimensions: Wing span 28ft 6½in *8.70m*;

length 19ft 2in *5.84m*.
Weights: Empty 904lb *410kg*; loaded 1322lb *600kg*.
Performance: Maximum speed 108.5mph *175kph*; time to 3280ft *1000m*,

3min; endurance 2.5hr.
Armament: One fixed machine gun.
Service: Service entry August 1917.

◄ **Port elevation**

Fuselage cross-sections ▼

▲ **Propeller**

Scale
0 1 2 3 4 5 6 7 8 ft
0 1 2 m

◄ Swiss Hanriot preserved by the Air Force, on show at Dubendorf, is in original condition. The RAF Museum example is restored in Belgian markings after travelling the world under mixed ownerships, as OO-APJ and G-AFDX, and also on the US civil register. (M Rutherford)

DRAWN BY P L GRAY

Colour notes
Belgian aircraft: Camouflaged on top and vertical surfaces (including cowl and metal panels) in large 'shadow-shaded' patches of dark green and khaki, with cream or very pale blue undersurfaces. Near full-chord roundels of black (centre), yellow and red were applied to the wing surfaces but not to the fuselage. Coppens flew Hanriots No 2, 6, 9, 17, 23, 24 and 45; No 6 was painted turquoise blue all over on 18 June 1918 and No 23 was similarly painted at a later date.
Italian aircraft: Uncamouflaged – clear doped linen overall; metal panels and cowling usually polished. Red (centre), white and green roundels on wing tips and fuselage sides.
American aircraft: Battleship grey fuselage, aluminium wings and tail. Roundels on wings only – white (centre), blue and red – and large white serial on fuselage sides.

Plan view
▼

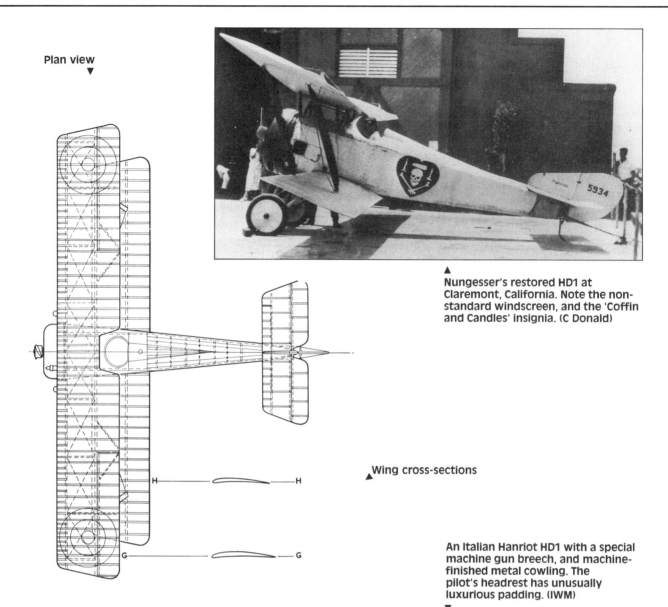

▲
Nungesser's restored HD1 at Claremont, California. Note the non-standard windscreen, and the 'Coffin and Candles' insignia. (C Donald)

H——————H

▲Wing cross-sections

G——————G

An Italian Hanriot HD1 with a special machine gun breech, and machine-finished metal cowling. The pilot's headrest has unusually luxurious padding. (IWM)
▼

HD1 of the Swiss Air Service with a white Greek cross on a scarlet square at wing tips and on rudder. (J Garwood)

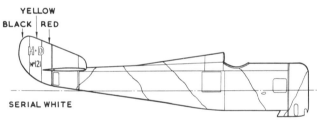

YELLOW
BLACK | RED

H·D
N°121

SERIAL WHITE

NO FUSELAGE ROUNDEL

▲ Scrap starboard elevation
Belgian camouflage pattern

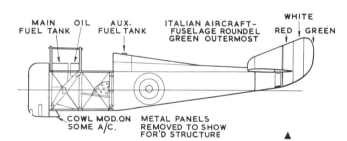

MAIN FUEL TANK   OIL   AUX. FUEL TANK   ITALIAN AIRCRAFT— FUSELAGE ROUNDEL GREEN OUTERMOST   WHITE   RED | GREEN

COWL MOD. ON SOME A/C.   METAL PANELS REMOVED TO SHOW FOR'D STRUCTURE

▲ Scrap view
Structure

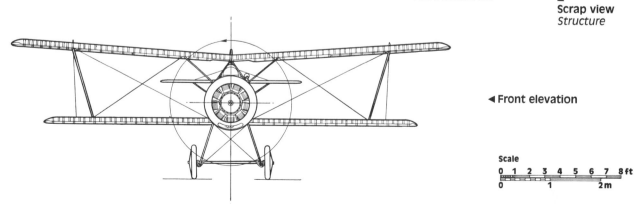

◄ Front elevation

Scale
0 1 2 3 4 5 6 7 8 ft
0   1   2 m

Albatros B I

Country of origin: Germany.
Type: Two-seat reconnaissance and training aircraft.
Powerplant: One Mercedes D I engine rated at 100hp or D II rated at 110hp.

Dimensions: Wing span 47ft 6in *14.48m*; length 25ft 1½in *7.60m*; height 10ft 4in *3.15m*.
Weights: Empty 1647lb *747kg*; loaded 2381lb *1080kg*.

Performance: Maximum speed 65mph *105kph*; time to 2600ft *800m*, 10min; endurance about 4hr.
Armament: None.
Service: Service entry August 1914.

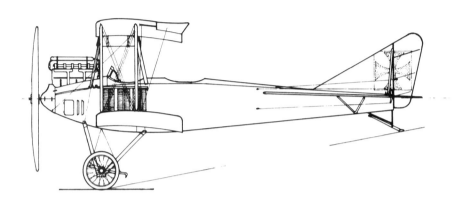

▲
Port elevation

Scrap starboard elevation ▶

DRAWN BY IAN R STAIR

Albatros B I with Mercedes engine. Designed and built before the war, this aircraft was pressed into reconnaissance and schooling duties in small numbers in August 1914. Both one and two-bay variants existed.
(H Woodman)
▼

Notes
Drawings show typical late military B I three-bay biplane; early prewar types had a different tail unit and parallel-chord ailerons. There was much variation of detail on B Is. The aircraft was also manufactured as a two-bay type similar in appearance to the B II.

Colour notes
Fuselage varnished plywood, dark-stained or natural. Wings and tail surfaces clear doped fabric. Insignia consisted of a black cross on a white panel on both surfaces of both wings and on fin/rudder. Proportions varied – on some aircraft the crosses were the same size as the panel – while the fin and rudder could be all white.

The Albatros B I reached its peak of operational use in April 1915 when 160 aircraft of the type are reported as being with front-line units. (A Imrie)

Scale

0 1 2 3 4 5 6 7 8 ft

0 1 2 m

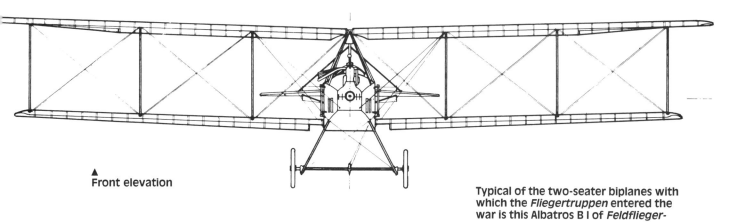

▲
Front elevation

Typical of the two-seater biplanes with which the *Fliegertruppen* entered the war is this Albatros B I of *Feldflieger-abteilung 23*. (A Imrie)
▼

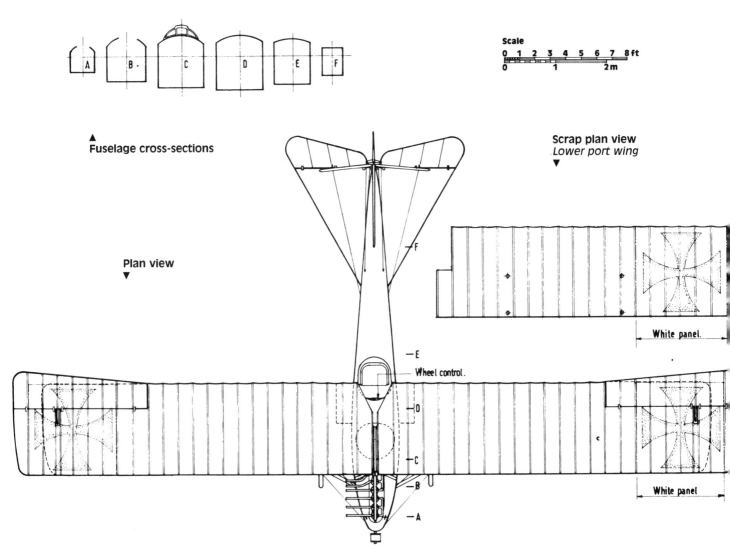

▲ **Fuselage cross-sections**

A B C D E F

Scrap plan view
Lower port wing
▼

White panel.

White panel

Plan view
▼

— E

— Wheel control.

— D

— C

— B

— A

c

**Albatros B I in the winter of 1914/15.
Cross patée is printed on both surfaces
of each wing panel on this triple bay
machine. (H Woodman)**
▼

Scale
0 1 2 3 4 5 6 7 8 ft
0 1 2 m

Albatros B II and IIa

Country of origin: Germany.
Type: Two-seat reconnaissance and training aircraft.
Powerplant: One Mercedes six-cylinder, liquid-cooled engine rated at 100hp, Benz Bz II rated at 110hp, Mercedes D II rated at 120hp or Argus As II rated at 120hp.

Dimensions: Wing span 42ft 0in *12.80m*, (IIa) 42ft 6¼in *12.96m*; length 25ft 0½in *7.63m*; height 10ft 4in *3.15m*; wing area 432 sq ft *40.12m²*, (IIa) 437.5 sq ft *40.64m²*.
Weights: Empty 1594lb *723kg*, (IIa) 1539lb *698kg*; loaded 2362lb *1071kg*, (IIa) 2377lb *1078kg*.

Performance: Maximum speed 65mph *105kph*, (IIa) 74.5mph *120kph*; time to 2625ft *800m*, 10min, (IIa) 8.2min; service ceiling 9850ft *3000m*; endurance 4hr.
Armament: None.
Service: Service entry 1914.

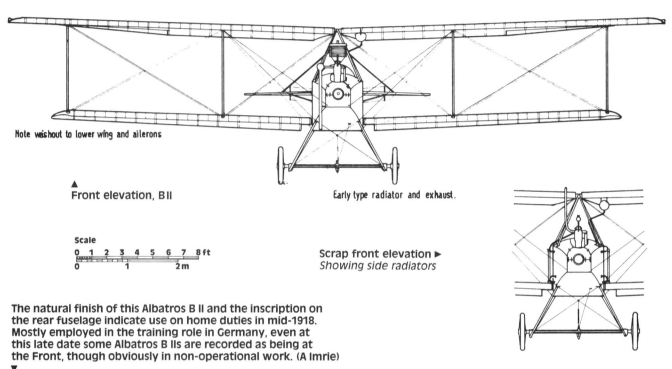

Note washout to lower wing and ailerons

▲
Front elevation, B II

Early type radiator and exhaust.

Scale
0 1 2 3 4 5 6 7 8 ft
0 1 2 m

Scrap front elevation ▶
Showing side radiators

The natural finish of this Albatros B II and the inscription on the rear fuselage indicate use on home duties in mid-1918. Mostly employed in the training role in Germany, even at this late date some Albatros B IIs are recorded as being at the Front, though obviously in non-operational work. (A Imrie)
▼

The Albatros B II was an
improved two-bay version
of the earlier B I and was
variously engined, being
produced by several sub-
contractors. It saw
widespread use, and 185 of
the type are recorded as
being at the Front by the
end of 1915. (A Imrie)
▼

Scale

0 1 2 3 4 5 6 7 8 ft
0   1   2 m

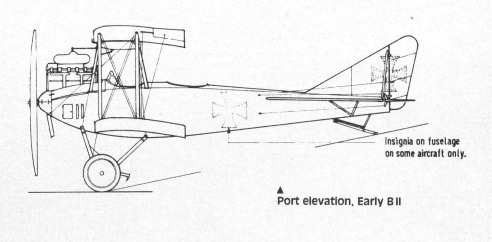

Insignia on fuselage
on some aircraft only.

▲
Port elevation, Early B II

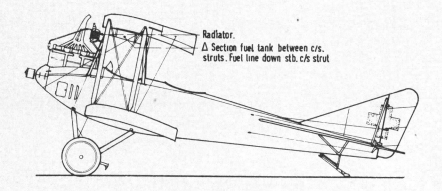

Radiator.
Δ Section fuel tank between c/s.
struts. Fuel line down stb. c/s strut

Notes
Wide-chord struts shown on elevation of
late B IIa were fitted by some contractors
but are not typical. Earlier B IIas usually had
side radiators as shown.

▲
Port elevation, Late B IIa

A bad landing! Note the early form of cross patée and the very distinctive triangular tail surface. (H Woodman) ▶

Scale

0 1 2 3 4 5 6 7 8 ft
0   1   2 m

▲
Propeller

Scrap starboard elevation ▶
Showing side radiators

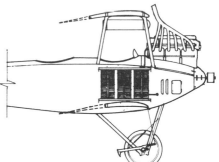

DETAIL OF SIDE RADIATORS Note number of sections could be varied to suit conditions

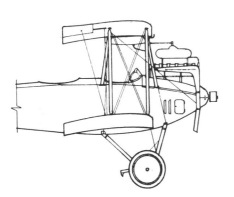

▲
Scrap starboard elevation, Early type

Albatros B II of *Feldfliegerabteilung 2*. Aircraft of this type were usually fitted with makeshift armament operated by the observer in the front seat and were used operationally until the spring of 1916. (A Imrie)
▼

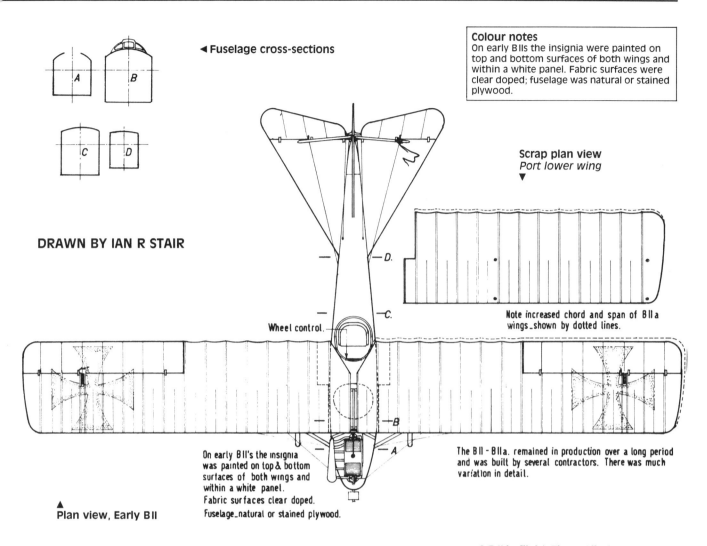

◄ **Fuselage cross-sections**

A B
C D

DRAWN BY IAN R STAIR

Colour notes
On early B IIs the insignia were painted on top and bottom surfaces of both wings and within a white panel. Fabric surfaces were clear doped; fuselage was natural or stained plywood.

Scrap plan view
Port lower wing
▼

Note increased chord and span of B II a wings shown by dotted lines.

_ D.

_ C.

Wheel control.

_ B

_ A

On early B II's the insignia was painted on top & bottom surfaces of both wings and within a white panel.
Fabric surfaces clear doped.
Fuselage natural or stained plywood.

The B II - B II a. remained in production over a long period and was built by several contractors. There was much variation in detail.

▲
Plan view, Early B II

A B II in flight. These Albatroses operated on reconnaissance duty well into 1915. (H Woodman)
▼

Albatros C V/16 and 17

Country of origin: Germany.
Type: Two-seat general-purpose aircraft.
Powerplant: One Mercedes D IV eight-cylinder, liquid-cooled engine rated at 220hp.
Dimensions: Wing span 41ft 11¼in

12.78m, (17) 41ft 5in 12.62m; length 29ft 4½in 8.95m; height 14ft 9¼in 4.50m; wing area 467.1 sq ft 43.4m².
Weights: Empty 2258lb 1024kg; loaded 3495lb 1585kg.
Performance: Maximum speed 105.5mph 170kph; time to 3280ft 1000m,

8min; endurance 3.25hr.
Armament: One fixed Spandau machine gun plus one flexibly mounted Parabellum machine gun.
Service: First flight: 1916.

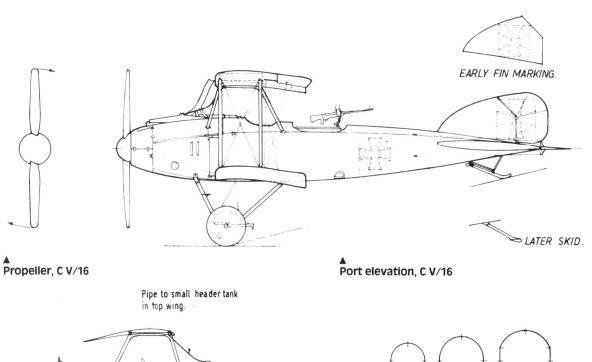

EARLY FIN MARKING.

LATER SKID.

▲
Propeller, C V/16

▲
Port elevation, C V/16

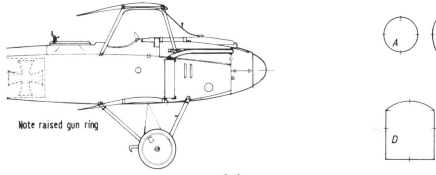

Pipe to small header tank in top wing.

Note raised gun ring

Scrap starboard elevation ▲
Later type with side exhaust

Scale
0 1 2 3 4 5 6 7 8 ft
0   1   2m

▲
Fuselage cross-sections, C V/16

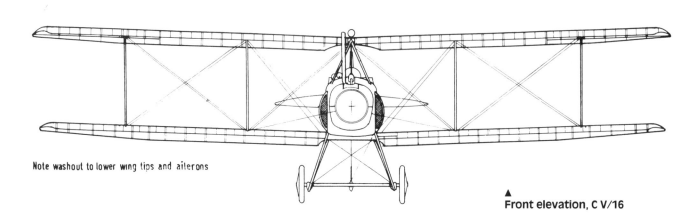

Note washout to lower wing tips and ailerons

▲
Front elevation, C V/16

▲
Final version of the Albatros C V, showing the radiator in the top wing centre-section. Note the claw brake on the undercarriage spreader bar – standard equipment on German two-seaters. Some 60 aircraft of this type were at the Front from mid-1916 until mid-1917. (A Imrie)

Colour notes
Fuselage and fin – plywood stained brown and varnished. Metal cowling, struts etc – light grey. Wings and horizontal tail surfaces – clear doped fabric. Top surfaces were later camouflaged in dark olive green ('G' on drawing) and rusty brown or lilac ('L'). Pattern shown is typical but varied according to aircraft.

Scrap plan view, C V/16
Forward fuselage
▼

Scrap plan view, C V/16
Port lower wing
▼

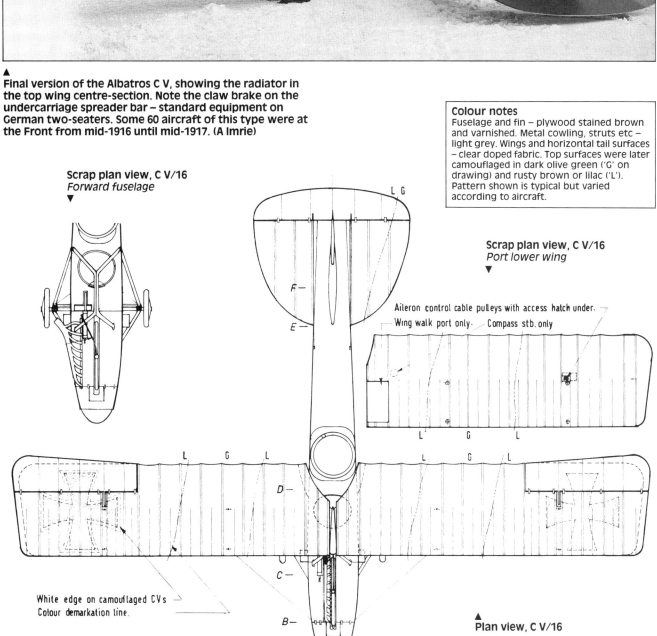

Aileron control cable pulleys with access hatch under.
Wing walk port only.   Compass stb. only

White edge on camouflaged CVs
Colour demarkation line.

▲ **Plan view, C V/16**

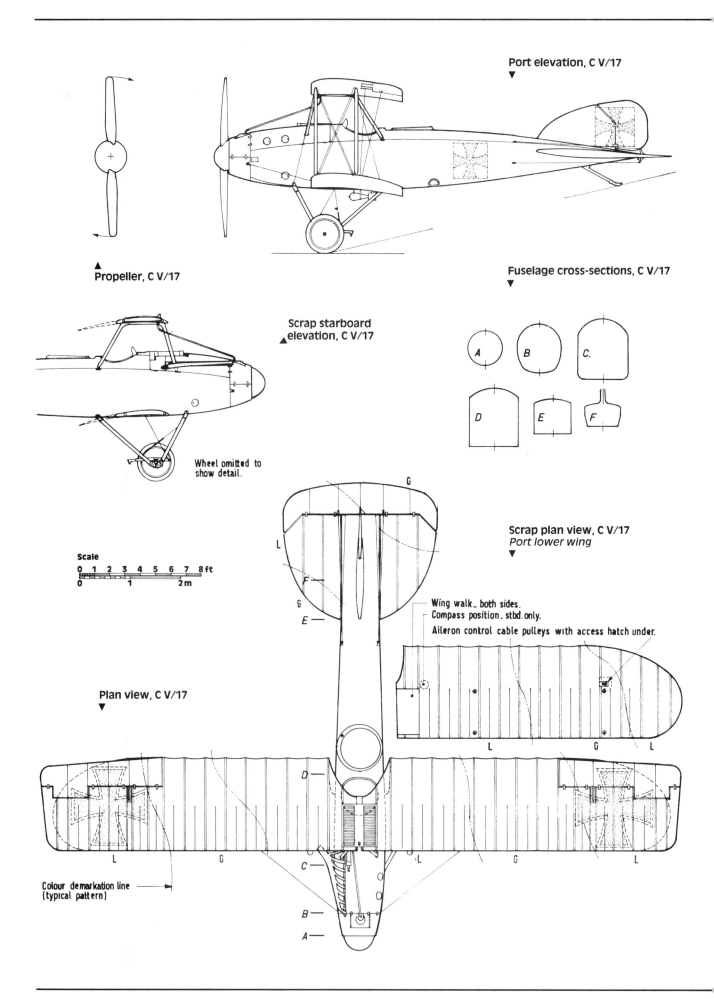

Port elevation, C V/17
▼

Propeller, C V/17
▲

Scrap starboard
▲ elevation, C V/17

Fuselage cross-sections, C V/17
▼

Wheel omitted to
show detail.

Scale

0 1 2 3 4 5 6 7 8 ft
0   1   2 m

Scrap plan view, C V/17
Port lower wing
▼

Wing walk _ both sides.
Compass position. stbd. only.

Aileron control cable pulleys with access hatch under.

Plan view, C V/17
▼

Colour demarkation line
(typical pattern)

▲ A clear view of a captured CV/17 which was brought down by AA fire near Armentiers in 1917. (H Woodman)

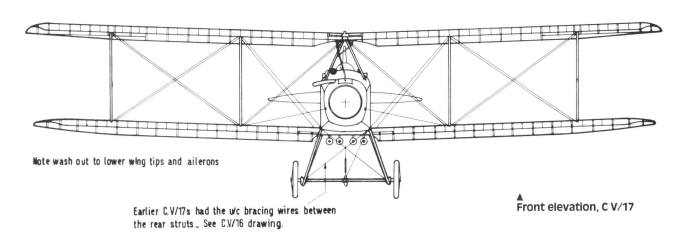

Note wash out to lower wing tips and ailerons

Earlier C.V/17s had the u/c bracing wires between the rear struts. See C.V/16 drawing.

▲ Front elevation, C V/17

Colour notes

Fuselage and fin were plywood, stained brown and varnished. Metal cowling, struts etc were light grey. Wings and tail surfaces (except fin) were clear doped on the undersurfaces, the uppersurfaces being camouflaged in dark olive green and lilac. One captured CV/17 (No G37) was camouflaged with random patches of dull greyish-green, dark green and brown.

Albatros C V of *Fliegerabteilung 2* about to make a three-point landing. The enormous geared propeller of its eight-cylinder, 220hp Mercedes engine is just idling. (H Woodman) ▶

Albatros D III

Country of origin: Germany.
Type: Single-seat scout.
Powerplant: One Mercedes D IIIa six-cylinder, liquid-cooled engine rated at 160hp (later uprated to 170–175hp).
Dimensions: Wing span 29ft 8¼in 9.05m; length 24ft 0½in 7.33m; height 9ft 9¼in 2.98m; wing area 220.7 sq ft 20.5m².
Weights: Empty 1457lb 661kg; loaded 1954lb 886kg.
Performance: Maximum speed 102.5mph 165kph; time to 3280ft 1000m, 4min; service ceiling 18,000ft 5485m; endurance 2hr.
Armament: Two fixed Spandau machine guns.
Service: Service entry early 1917.

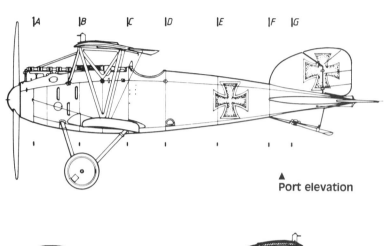

▲ Port elevation

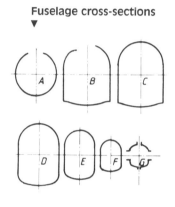

Fuselage cross-sections
▼

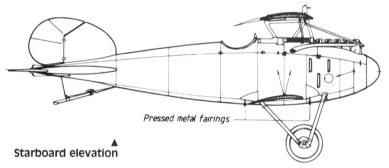

Pressed metal fairings

▲ Starboard elevation

An Albatros D III from a batch constructed by the OAW Albatros subsidiary, interned in Switzerland and displaying the Balkenkreuz (straight-sided) national insignia, changed from the Iron Cross from March 1918.
▼

▲
Immaculately finished in white dope, this Albatros D III has just been completely overhauled for use by members of ZAK (*Zentral Abnahme Kommission*), the authority for aircraft acceptance, to speed travel between aircraft factories. (A Imrie)

Scrap plan view
Wing omitted
▼

Colour notes
Factory finish comprised varnished plywood fuselage and fin; light grey or olive green cowling panels, struts and metal fittings; large, irregular patches of dark olive green and lilac (hazy edges) on upper surfaces of wings and tailplane; pale blue undersurfaces; and white rudder (or as upper surfaces). Lozenge fabric appeared on some late D IIIs.

Plan view
▼

DRAWN BY IAN R STAIR

Plywood leading edge, top surface only.

CENTRAL RADIATOR ON EARLY D IIIs.

▲
Scrap plan view

Wing cross-sections
▼

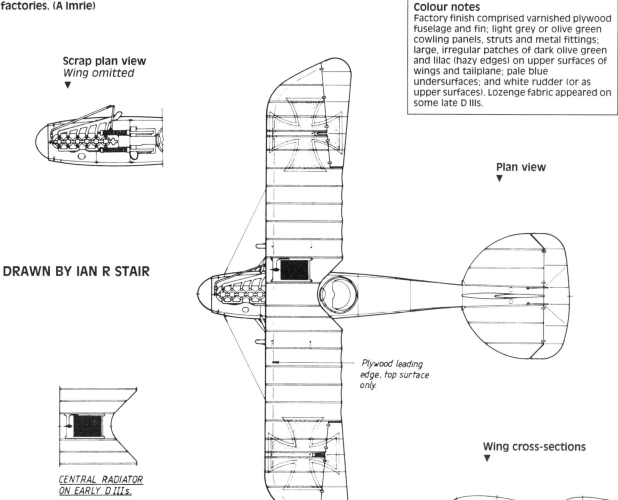

▲
Following the aircraft's type test in September 1916, 400
Albatros D IIIs were ordered. This machine reigned supreme
over the Western Front in the spring of 1917. (A Imrie)

Front elevation
▼

Scrap underplan
Wing centre-section
▼

Shutters
Operating lever

Washout, lower wing tips and ailerons.

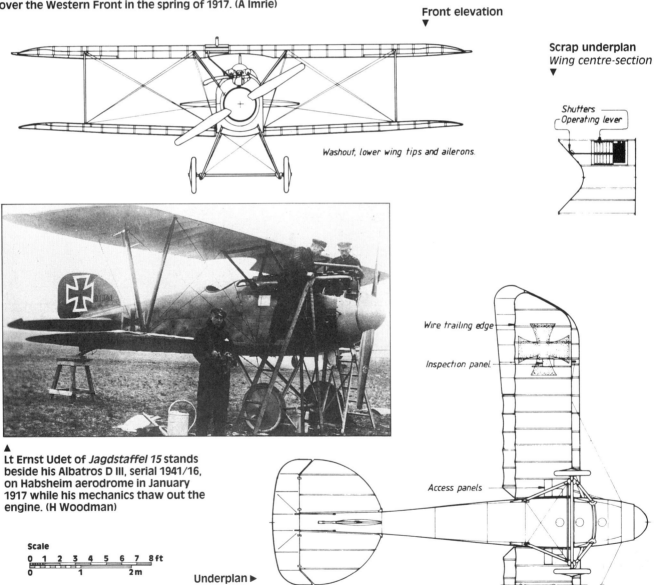

▲
Lt Ernst Udet of *Jagdstaffel 15* stands
beside his Albatros D III, serial 1941/16,
on Habsheim aerodrome in January
1917 while his mechanics thaw out the
engine. (H Woodman)

Wire trailing edge

Inspection panel

Access panels

Scale
0 1 2 3 4 5 6 7 8 ft
0   1   2 m

Underplan ▶

Albatros J I

Country of origin: Germany.
Type: Two-seat close-support aircraft.
Powerplant: One Benz Bz IV six-cylinder, liquid-cooled engine rated at 200hp.
Dimensions: Wing span 46ft 4¾in *14.14m*; length 28ft 11¾in *8.83m*; height

11ft 0¾in *3.37m*; wing area 460.9 sq ft *42.82m²*.
Weights: Empty 3083lb *1398kg*; loaded 3987lb *1808kg*.
Performance: Maximum speed 87mph *140kph*; time to 3280ft *1000m*, 11.4min;

endurance 2.5hr.
Armament: Two fixed Spandau machine guns and one flexibly mounted Parabellum machine gun.
Service: Service entry autumn 1917.

Port elevation ▼

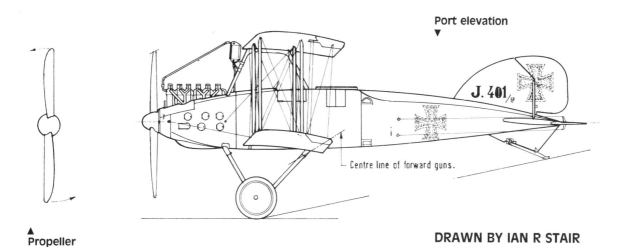

▲ Propeller

DRAWN BY IAN R STAIR

Note washout on ailerons. both wings.

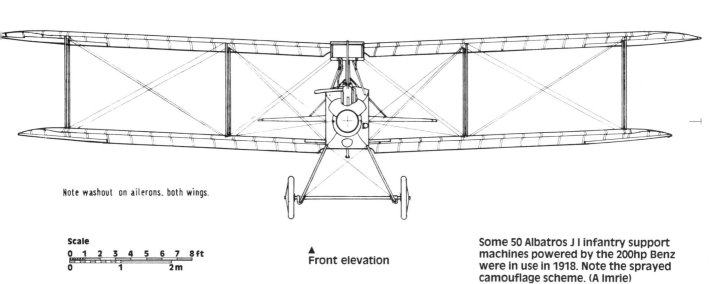

Scale

```
0  1  2  3  4  5  6  7  8 ft
0           1          2 m
```

▲ Front elevation

Some 50 Albatros J I infantry support machines powered by the 200hp Benz were in use in 1918. Note the sprayed camouflage scheme. (A Imrie) ▼

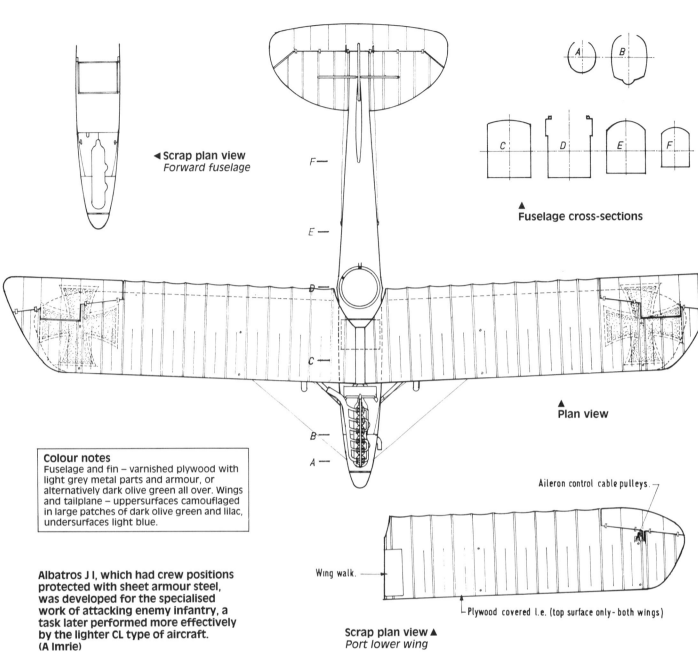

◄ **Scrap plan view**
Forward fuselage

F —

E —

D —

C —

B —

A —

▲ **Fuselage cross-sections**

▲ **Plan view**

Colour notes
Fuselage and fin – varnished plywood with light grey metal parts and armour, or alternatively dark olive green all over. Wings and tailplane – uppersurfaces camouflaged in large patches of dark olive green and lilac, undersurfaces light blue.

Aileron control cable pulleys.

Wing walk.

Plywood covered l.e. (top surface only - both wings)

Scrap plan view ▲
Port lower wing

Albatros J I, which had crew positions protected with sheet armour steel, was developed for the specialised work of attacking enemy infantry, a task later performed more effectively by the lighter CL type of aircraft. (A Imrie)
▼

Albatros J II

Country of origin: Germany.
Type: Two-seat close-support and reconnaissance aircraft.
Powerplant: One Benz Bz IVa engine rated at 220hp.
Dimensions: Wing span 44ft 5½in

13.55m; length 27ft 8in *8.43m*; height 11ft 1¾in *3.40m*; wing area 465 sq ft *43.2m²*.
Weights: Empty 2265lb *1027kg*; loaded 4249lb *1927kg*.
Performance: Maximum speed 87mph

140kph; time to 3280ft *1000m*, 8.7min; endurance 2.5hr.
Armament: Two fixed machine guns and one flexibly mounted Parabellum machine gun.
Service: First flight 1918.

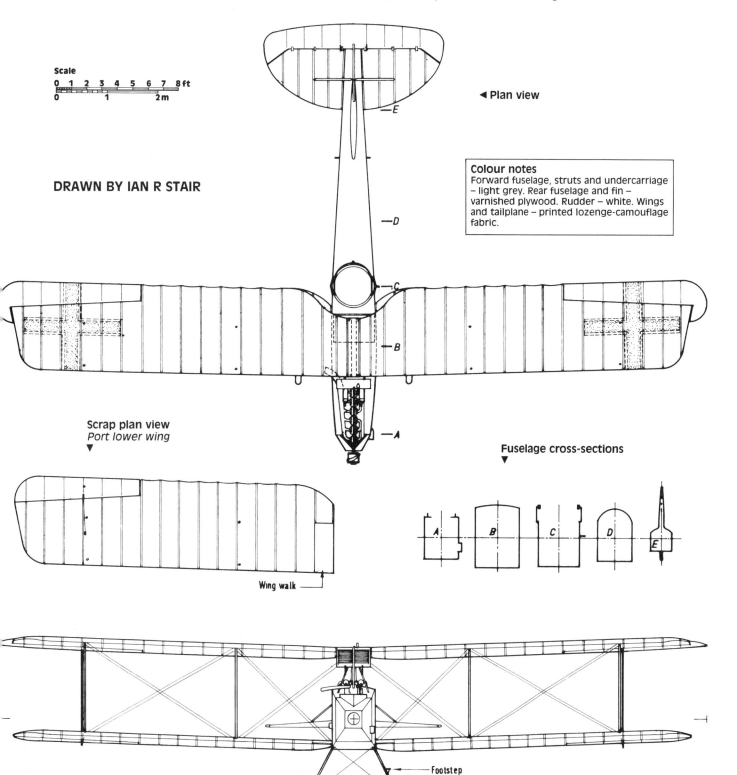

Scale
0 1 2 3 4 5 6 7 8 ft
0   1   2m

◄ Plan view

DRAWN BY IAN R STAIR

Colour notes
Forward fuselage, struts and undercarriage – light grey. Rear fuselage and fin – varnished plywood. Rudder – white. Wings and tailplane – printed lozenge-camouflage fabric.

Scrap plan view
Port lower wing
▼

Fuselage cross-sections
▼

Wing walk

Footstep

▲ Front elevation

▲
The Albatros J II, a more heavily armoured update of the J I.
(H Woodman)

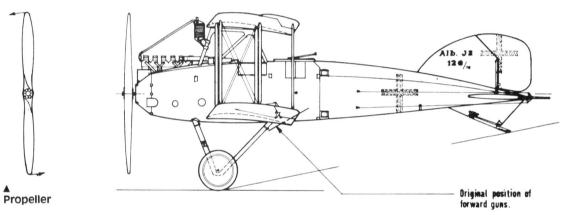

▲
Propeller

Original position of
forward guns.

The J II was an improved version of J I, having sheet armour
steel over the whole nose area to protect the engine and
fuel tanks as well as the crew. Twenty machines were at
the Front in August 1918. (A Imrie)

▲
Port elevation

▼

DFW C V

Country of origin: Germany.
Type: Two-seat reconnaissance, observation and patrol aircraft.
Powerplant: One Benz Bz IV six-cylinder, liquid-cooled engine rated at 200hp.
Dimensions: Wing span 43ft 6½in

13.27m; length 25ft 10in *7.87m*; height 10ft 8in *3.25m*.
Weights: Empty 2139lb *970kg*; loaded 3153lb *1430kg*.
Performance: Maximum speed 96.25mph *155kph*; time to 3280ft *1000m*,

4min; service ceiling 16,400ft *5000m*; endurance 3.5hr.
Armament: One fixed Spandau machine gun and one flexibly mounted Parabellum machine gun.
Service: Service entry late 1916.

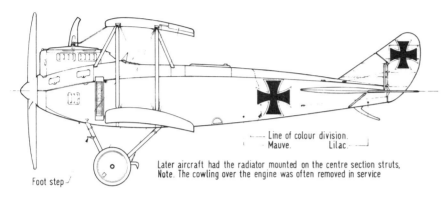

◄ **Port elevation**
Note side radiators

--- Line of colour division.
Mauve.   Lilac.

Later aircraft had the radiator mounted on the centre section struts.
Note. The cowling over the engine was often removed in service

Foot step

Port elevation, Late production aircraft
Aviatik-built, drawn as in service with Fl Abt 287
▼

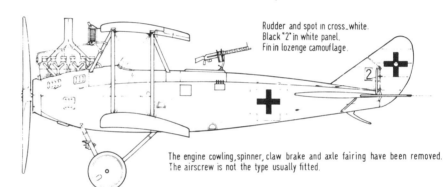

Rudder and spot in cross white.
Black "2" in white panel.
Fin in lozenge camouflage.

The engine cowling, spinner, claw brake and axle fairing have been removed.
The airscrew is not the type usually fitted.

▲
Scrap port elevation
Aileron control detail

Scale
0 1 2 3 4 5 6 7 8ft
0   1   2m

The DFW C V was introduced in the autumn of 1916, over 1000 were in front-line use in August 1917, and the type continued to serve until the Armistice. Seen on Bellincamps aerodrome on 22 May 1917 is machine '3' of *Fliegerabteilung (A) 224*. (A Imrie)
▼

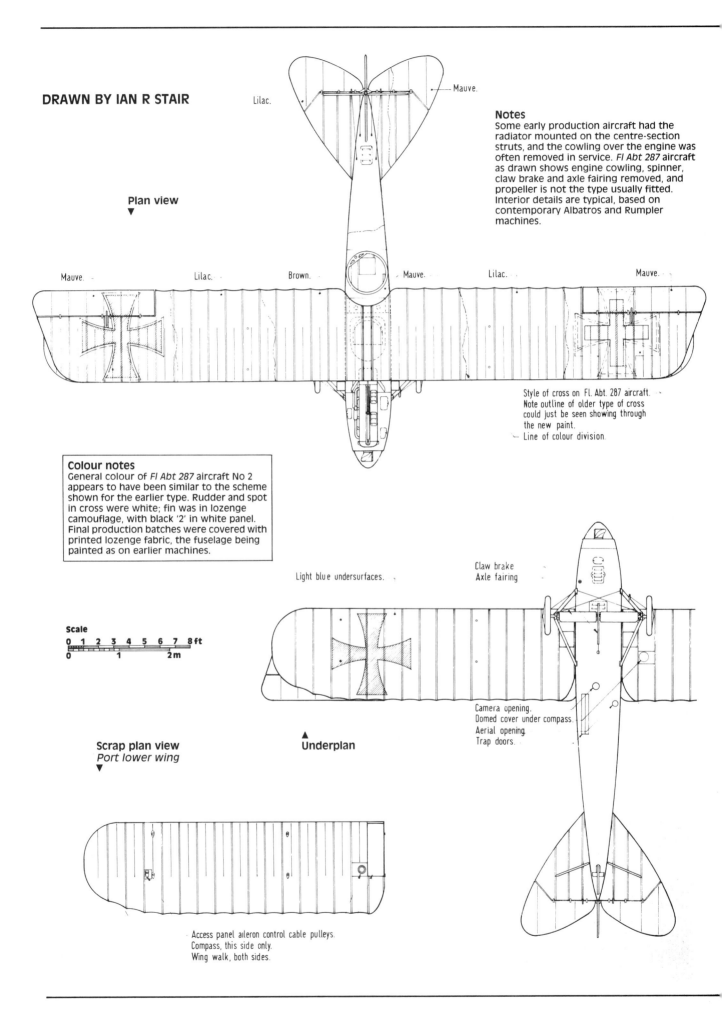

DRAWN BY IAN R STAIR

Lilac.

Mauve.

Plan view
▼

Notes
Some early production aircraft had the radiator mounted on the centre-section struts, and the cowling over the engine was often removed in service. *Fl Abt 287* aircraft as drawn shows engine cowling, spinner, claw brake and axle fairing removed, and propeller is not the type usually fitted. Interior details are typical, based on contemporary Albatros and Rumpler machines.

Mauve.   Lilac.   Brown.   Mauve.   Lilac.   Mauve.

Style of cross on Fl. Abt. 287 aircraft.
Note outline of older type of cross could just be seen showing through the new paint.
— Line of colour division.

Colour notes
General colour of *Fl Abt 287* aircraft No 2 appears to have been similar to the scheme shown for the earlier type. Rudder and spot in cross were white; fin was in lozenge camouflage, with black '2' in white panel. Final production batches were covered with printed lozenge fabric, the fuselage being painted as on earlier machines.

Light blue undersurfaces.

Claw brake
Axle fairing

Scale
0 1 2 3 4 5 6 7 8 ft
0   1   2 m

Scrap plan view
Port lower wing
▼

▲
Underplan

Camera opening.
Domed cover under compass.
Aerial opening.
Trap doors.

Access panel aileron control cable pulleys.
Compass, this side only.
Wing walk, both sides.

▲ The C V was the most widely used general purpose two-seater during the last two years of the war. This one was employed in 1919 on courier flights between Nürnberg and Munich. (A Imrie)

▲ An overview of a DFW C V displays the mottle-sprayed camouflage scheme. (H Woodman)

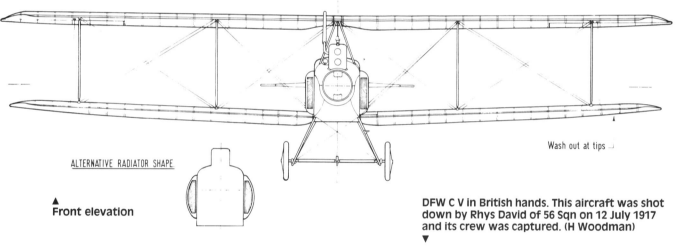

Wash out at tips ⌐

ALTERNATIVE RADIATOR SHAPE.

▲ Front elevation

DFW C V in British hands. This aircraft was shot down by Rhys David of 56 Sqn on 12 July 1917 and its crew was captured. (H Woodman)
▼

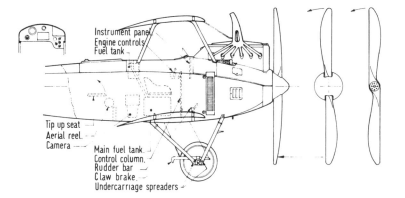

Instrument panel
Engine controls
Fuel tank

Tip up seat
Aerial reel.
Camera
Main fuel tank.
Control column.
Rudder bar
Claw brake.
Undercarriage spreaders

◄ Scrap starboard elevation

Fuselage cross-sections
▼

NOTE. Interior details are typical, based on contemporary
Albatros and Rumpler aircraft.

**Scrap front elevation, Late production
aircraft ▼**

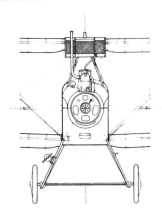

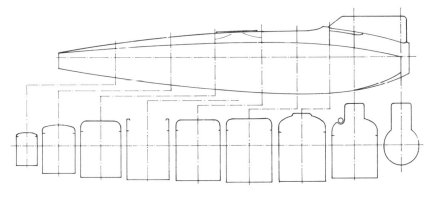

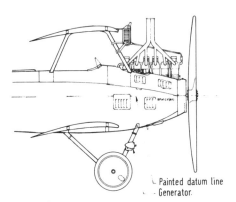

Painted datum line
Generator.

▲
Scrap starboard elevation, Late
production aircraft

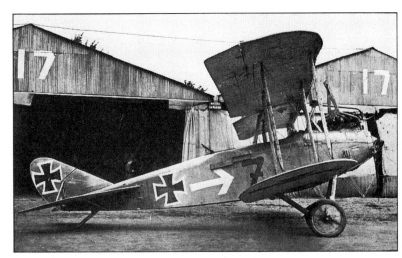

**Another view of the captured DFW C V,
which was given the British number
G35. (H Woodman) ►▲**

**The cockpit of a captured, Aviatik-built DFW C
V (Av): C5927/16 was fitted with some British
instruments and tested as aircraft G24 at
Martlesham Heath in 1917. (J M Bruce/
G S Leslie) ►**

Scale
0 1 2 3 4 5 6 7 8 ft
0   1   2 m

Fokker D VII

Country of origin: Germany.
Type: Single-seat scout.
Powerplant: One Mercedes six-cylinder engine rated at 160hp, 180hp, 200hp or 220hp or BMW rated at 185hp.
Dimensions: Wing span 29ft 3½in *8.93m*; length 23ft 0in *7.01m*; height 9ft 3in *2.82m*; wing area 236 sq ft *21.92m²*.

Weights: (160hp Mercedes) Empty 1540lb *698kg*; loaded 1936lb *878kg*.
Performance: Maximum speed (160hp Mercedes) 120mph *193kph* at sea level, (BMW) 124mph *200kph* at sea level, (220hp Mercedes) 135mph *217.5kph* at sea level; time to 3280ft *1000m* (160hp Mercedes), 4.25min; service ceiling

(160hp Mercedes) 18,000ft *5485m*, (BMW) 21,000ft *6400m*.
Armament: Two fixed Spandau machine guns.
Service: First flight late 1917; service entry May 1918.

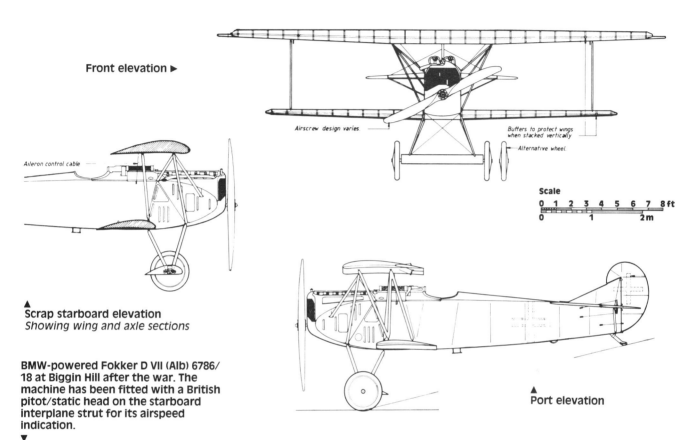

Front elevation ►

Airscrew design varies.

Buffers to protect wings when stacked vertically

Alternative wheel.

Aileron control cable

▲
Scrap starboard elevation
Showing wing and axle sections

Scale

▲
Port elevation

BMW-powered Fokker D VII (Alb) 6786/ 18 at Biggin Hill after the war. The machine has been fitted with a British pitot/static head on the starboard interplane strut for its airspeed indication.
▼

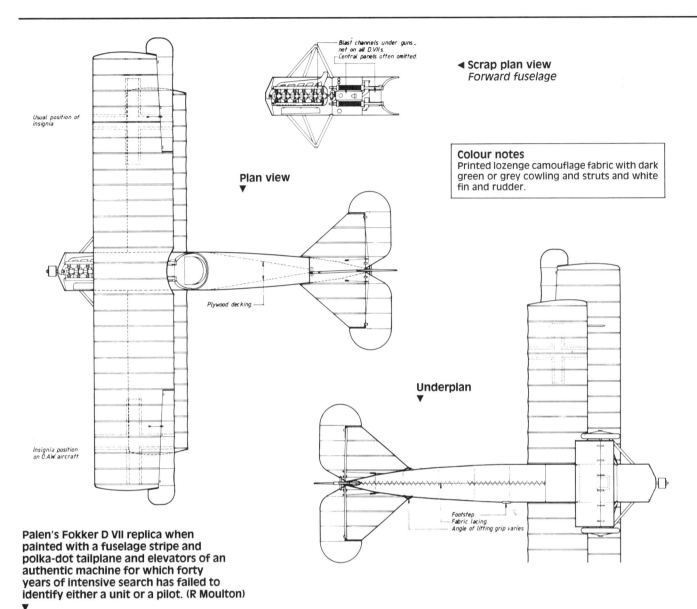

Usual position of insignia

Blast channels under guns
not on all D.VII s.
Central panels often omitted.

◀ **Scrap plan view**
Forward fuselage

Plan view
▼

Colour notes
Printed lozenge camouflage fabric with dark green or grey cowling and struts and white fin and rudder.

Plywood decking

Underplan
▼

Insignia position on O.A.W. aircraft

Footstep
Fabric lacing
Angle of lifting grip varies

Palen's Fokker D VII replica when painted with a fuselage stripe and polka-dot tailplane and elevators of an authentic machine for which forty years of intensive search has failed to identify either a unit or a pilot. (R Moulton)
▼

Fuselage cross-sections
▼

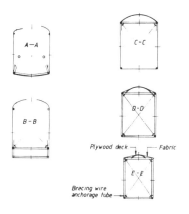

A-A

C-C

B-B

D-D

Plywood deck — — Fabric

E-E

Bracing wire
anchorage tube

▲
The Fokker D VII replica flown at Old Rhinebeck is painted to imitate D VII 286/18 flown by *Vizefeldwebel* Gabriel in *Jagdstaffel 11*, with lozenge-pattern wings, streaked fuselage and tailplane striped in orange and light blue. (E van Gorder)

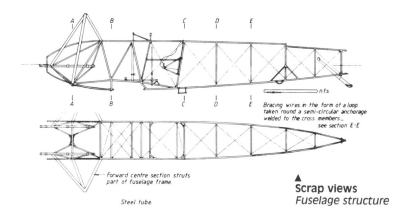

n.t.s.

Bracing wires in the form of a loop
taken round a semi-circular anchorage
welded to the cross members.
see section E-E

Forward centre section struts
part of fuselage frame.

Steel tube.

▲
Scrap views
Fuselage structure

DRAWN BY IAN R STAIR

Wing cross-sections
At tips
▼

Notes
Drawings depict a typical late Fokker-built aircraft with a 180hp Mercedes engine. Cowling details varied with different batches and with individual sub-contractors. Wings were built with wing spars straight on the top edge, but owing to the change in rib contour the top surface of the wing was about ½in higher at the centre section than at the tips. This dimension would vary according to whether the machine was on the ground or flying, because of flexing.

Scrap views ▶
Wing structure

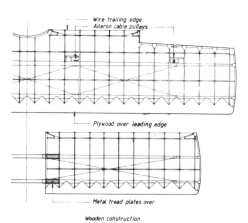

Wire trailing edge
Aileron cable pulleys

Plywood over leading edge

Metal tread plates over

Wooden construction.

Fokker Dr 1

Country of origin: Germany.
Type: Single-seat scout.
Powerplant: One Oberursel Ur II rotary engine rated at 110hp or Le Rhône rated at 110hp.
Dimensions: Wing span 23ft 7in *7.19m*; length 18ft 11in *5.77m*; height 9ft 8in

2.95m; wing area (inc axle) 200.8 sq ft *18.66m²*.
Weights: Empty 895lb *406kg*; loaded 1292lb *586kg*.
Performance: Maximum speed 102.5mph *165kph* at 13,120ft *4000m*; time to 3280ft *1000m*, 2.9min; service

ceiling 20,000ft *6100m*; endurance about 1.5hr.
Armament: Two fixed Spandau machine guns.
Service: Service entry summer 1917.

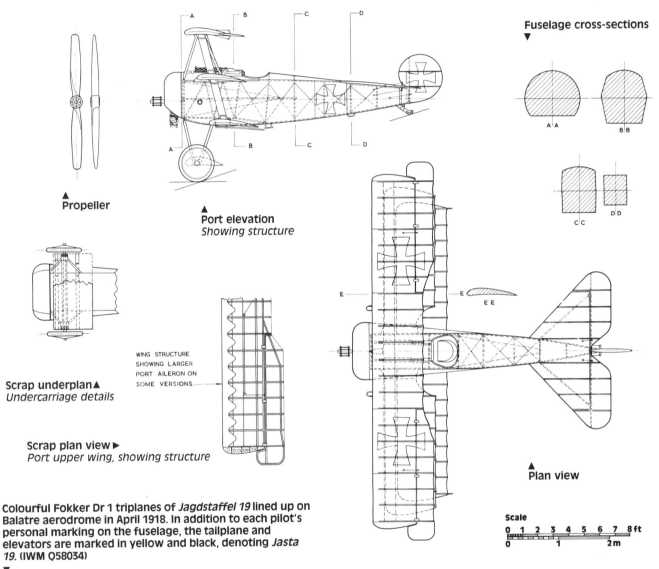

▲ **Propeller**

▲ **Port elevation**
Showing structure

Fuselage cross-sections
▼

A A   B B

C C   D D

Scrap underplan▲
Undercarriage details

WING STRUCTURE SHOWING LARGER PORT AILERON ON SOME VERSIONS.

Scrap plan view ▶
Port upper wing, showing structure

E E

▲ **Plan view**

Scale
0 1 2 3 4 5 6 7 8ft
0 1 2m

Colourful Fokker Dr 1 triplanes of *Jagdstaffel 19* lined up on Balatre aerodrome in April 1918. In addition to each pilot's personal marking on the fuselage, the tailplane and elevators are marked in yellow and black, denoting *Jasta 19*. (IWM Q58034)
▼

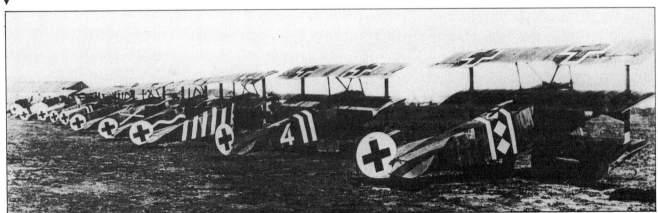

Front elevation
▼

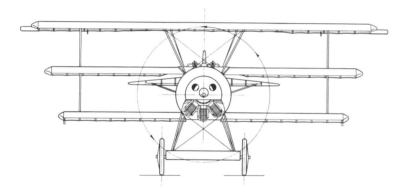

▲
One horsepower being used to move some 800lb of Fokker Dr 1 triplane of *Jagdstaffel 12* on a muddy Toulis aerodrome in March 1918. (E van Gorder)

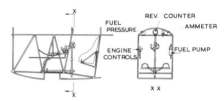

▲
Scrap views
Cockpit details

DRAWN BY P L GRAY

Not fully genuine, Cole Palen's Fokker triplane replica is one of many fascinating 'close' resemblances at his Old Rhinebeck airstrip in upper New York State. (R Moulton)
▼

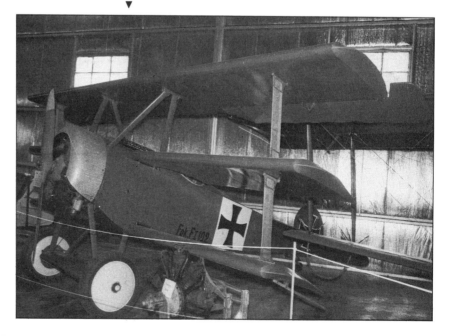

Colour notes

It would appear that Dr 1s first left the factory camouflaged in narrow streaks of dark greyish-green and lightish brown on the top and sides, and a pale sky blue underneath, until the introduction of colour-printed 'lozenge' fabric at a later date. When received by *Staffeln*, aircraft were considerably brightened up by the addition of coloured identity bands etc to fuselage and/or tail surfaces. Machines flown by von Richthofen were scarlet all over with the exception of the rudder, which was white; other aircraft of *11 Staffel* were mainly red, with white distinguishing marks added (e.g. the triplane of Reinhard had white stripes between alternate ribs on the tailplane). National insignia took the form of black patee crosses (later, in 1918, revised to Latin crosses), usually painted on a square white background or with a white outline. Serial numbers were painted near the bottom of the fuselage just aft of the cockpit (as on the D VIII) in black, but these were often obliterated by *Staffel* decor.

Gotha G IV and V

Country of origin: Germany.
Type: Three-seat long-range bomber.
Powerplant: Two Mercedes D IVa six-cylinder, liquid-cooled engines each rated at 260hp.
Dimensions: Wing span 77ft 9¼in *23.70m*; length 38ft 11in *11.86m*; height 14ft 1¼in *4.30m*; wing area 963.4 sq ft *89.5m²*.
Weights: Empty 5292lb *2400kg*, (G V) 6042lb *2740kg*; loaded 8015lb *3635kg*, (G V) 8765lb *3975kg*.
Performance: Maximum speed 87mph *140kph* at 12,000ft *3660m*; time to 9850ft *3000m*, 28min; service ceiling 21,325ft *6500m*; range 305 miles *490km*.
Armament: Bomb load up to 1100lb *500kg*, plus two flexibly mounted Parabellum machine guns.
Service: Service entry (G IV) autumn 1916.

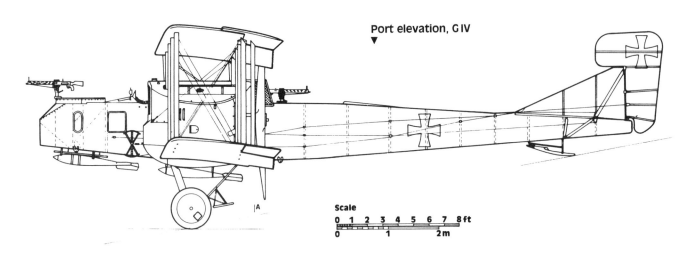

Port elevation, G IV ▼

Scale
0 1 2 3 4 5 6 7 8 ft
0 1 2m

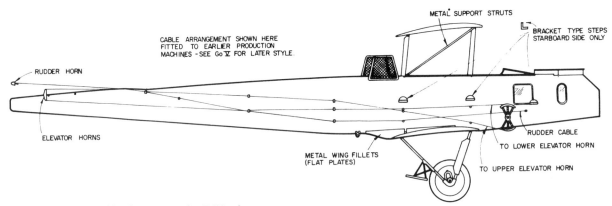

CABLE ARRANGEMENT SHOWN HERE FITTED TO EARLIER PRODUCTION MACHINES – SEE Go V FOR LATER STYLE.

METAL SUPPORT STRUTS

BRACKET TYPE STEPS STARBOARD SIDE ONLY

RUDDER HORN

ELEVATOR HORNS

METAL WING FILLETS (FLAT PLATES)

RUDDER CABLE
TO LOWER ELEVATOR HORN
TO UPPER ELEVATOR HORN

The Gotha G IV, powered by two Mercedes D IVa six-cylinder, 260hp engines driving pusher propellers, equipped the so-called '*England Geschwader*'. Thirty-six aircraft were operational by June 1917 against targets in south-east England. (A Imrie)
▼

▲
Scrap starboard elevation, G IV

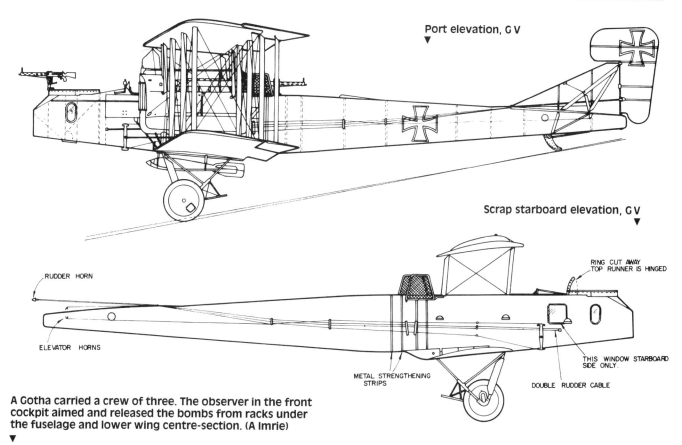

Port elevation, G V
▼

Scrap starboard elevation, G V
▼

RING CUT AWAY
TOP RUNNER IS HINGED

RUDDER HORN

ELEVATOR HORNS

THIS WINDOW STARBOARD
SIDE ONLY.

METAL STRENGTHENING
STRIPS

DOUBLE RUDDER CABLE

A Gotha carried a crew of three. The observer in the front
cockpit aimed and released the bombs from racks under
the fuselage and lower wing centre-section. (A Imrie)
▼

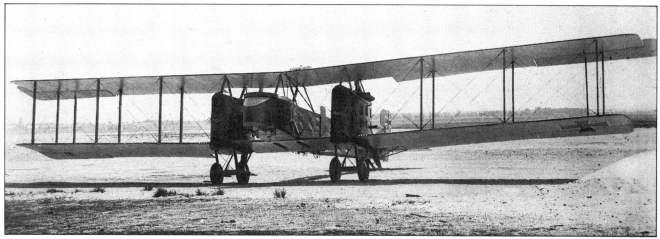

Scrap view, G IV
Structure
▼

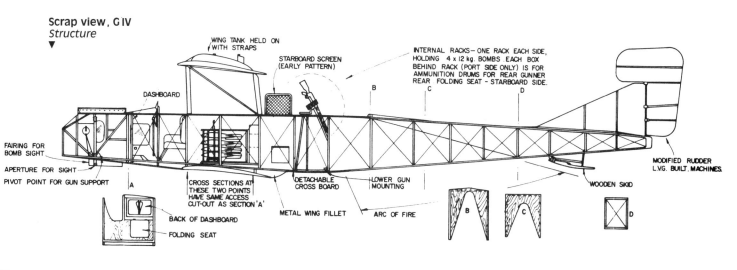

WING TANK HELD ON
WITH STRAPS

STARBOARD SCREEN
(EARLY PATTERN)

INTERNAL RACKS—ONE RACK EACH SIDE,
HOLDING 4 x 12 kg. BOMBS EACH BOX
BEHIND RACK (PORT SIDE ONLY) IS FOR
AMMUNITION DRUMS FOR REAR GUNNER
REAR FOLDING SEAT - STARBOARD SIDE.

DASHBOARD

B

C

D

FAIRING FOR
BOMB SIGHT

APERTURE FOR SIGHT

PIVOT POINT FOR GUN SUPPORT

A

CROSS SECTIONS AT
THESE TWO POINTS
HAVE SAME ACCESS
CUT-OUT AS SECTION 'A'

DETACHABLE
CROSS BOARD

LOWER GUN
MOUNTING

MODIFIED RUDDER
L.V.G. BUILT MACHINES.

WOODEN SKID

BACK OF DASHBOARD

FOLDING SEAT

METAL WING FILLET

ARC OF FIRE

B

C

D

▲
This overview of a Gotha shows the crew positions and connecting passages between the three cockpits. The early daylight raids on England made by these aircraft achieved considerable success, with an impressively low casualty rate. (H Woodman)

Scrap plan view, G IV
Port lower wing
▼

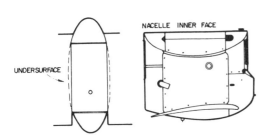

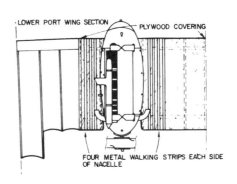

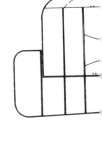

Scrap views, G V
▼

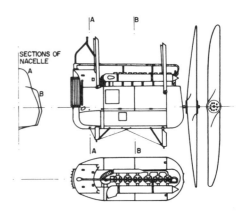

▲
Scrap views, G IV
Engine nacelle

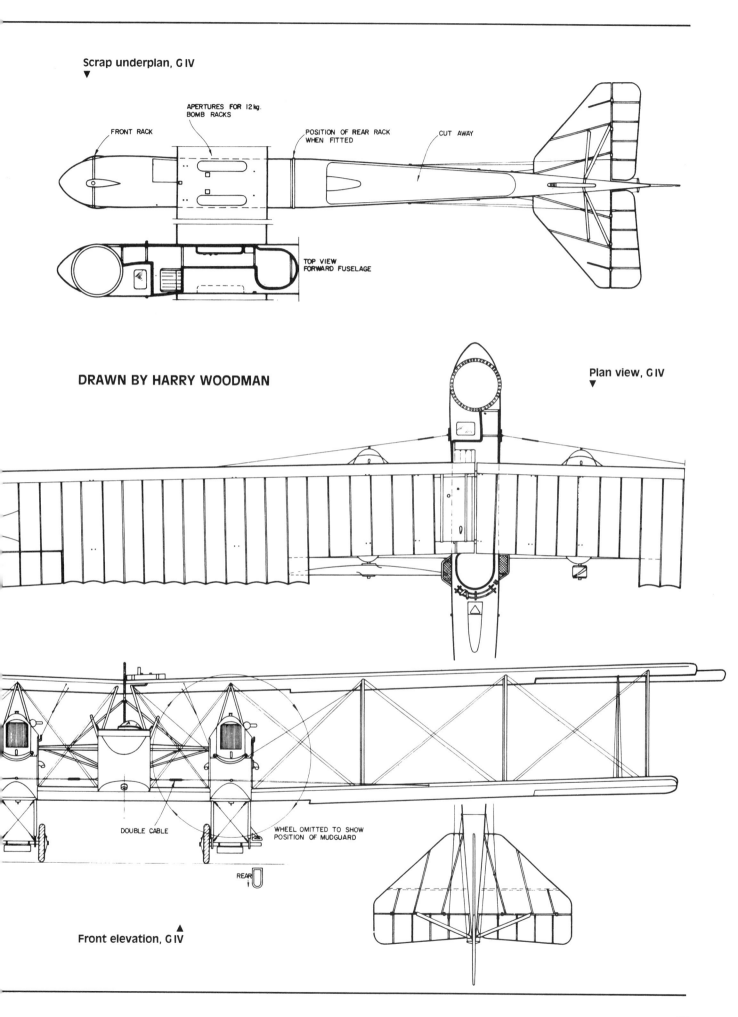

Scrap underplan, G IV

APERTURES FOR 12 kg.
BOMB RACKS

FRONT RACK

POSITION OF REAR RACK
WHEN FITTED

CUT AWAY

TOP VIEW
FORWARD FUSELAGE

DRAWN BY HARRY WOODMAN

Plan view, G IV

DOUBLE CABLE

WHEEL OMITTED TO SHOW
POSITION OF MUDGUARD

REAR

Front elevation, G IV

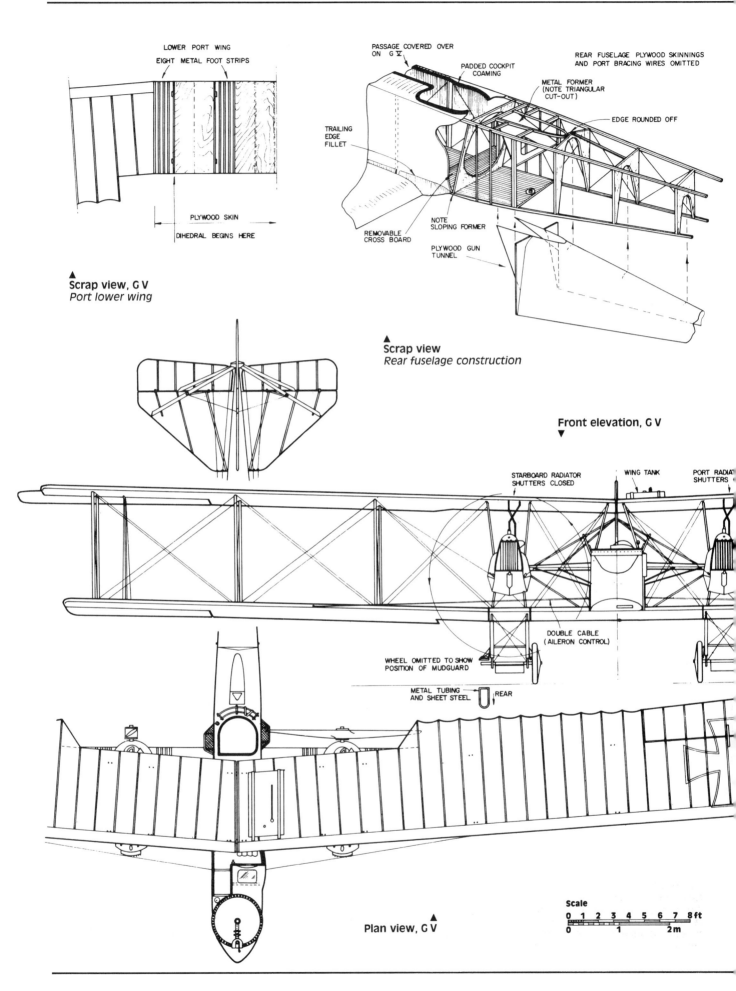

LOWER PORT WING

EIGHT METAL FOOT STRIPS

PLYWOOD SKIN

DIHEDRAL BEGINS HERE

Scrap view, G V
Port lower wing

PASSAGE COVERED OVER ON G V

PADDED COCKPIT COAMING

REAR FUSELAGE PLYWOOD SKINNINGS AND PORT BRACING WIRES OMITTED

METAL FORMER (NOTE TRIANGULAR CUT-OUT)

EDGE ROUNDED OFF

TRAILING EDGE FILLET

REMOVABLE CROSS BOARD

NOTE SLOPING FORMER

PLYWOOD GUN TUNNEL

Scrap view
Rear fuselage construction

Front elevation, G V

STARBOARD RADIATOR SHUTTERS CLOSED

WING TANK

PORT RADIAT SHUTTERS

DOUBLE CABLE (AILERON CONTROL)

WHEEL OMITTED TO SHOW POSITION OF MUDGUARD

METAL TUBING AND SHEET STEEL

REAR

Plan view, G V

Scale

0 1 2 3 4 5 6 7 8 ft

0 1 2m

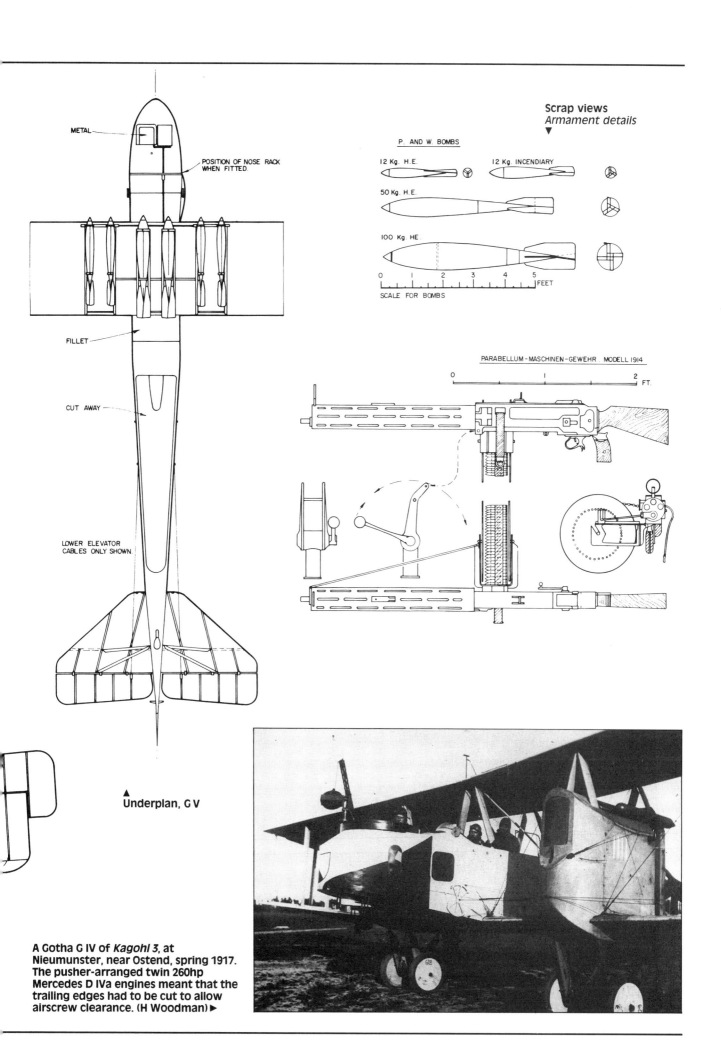

METAL

POSITION OF NOSE RACK WHEN FITTED.

FILLET

CUT AWAY

LOWER ELEVATOR CABLES ONLY SHOWN.

▲
Underplan, G V

Scrap views
Armament details
▼

P. AND W. BOMBS

12 Kg. H.E.

12 Kg. INCENDIARY

50 Kg. H.E.

100 Kg. HE.

0 1 2 3 4 5 FEET
SCALE FOR BOMBS

PARABELLUM-MASCHINEN-GEWEHR . MODELL 1914

0 1 2 FT.

A Gotha G IV of *Kagohl 3*, at Nieumunster, near Ostend, spring 1917. The pusher-arranged twin 260hp Mercedes D IVa engines meant that the trailing edges had to be cut to allow airscrew clearance. (H Woodman)▶

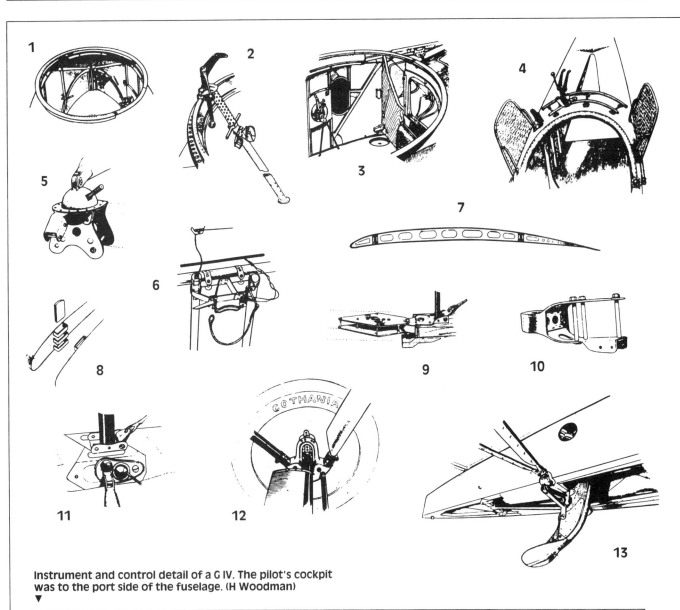

1

2

3

4

5

7

6

8

9

10

11

12

13

Instrument and control detail of a G IV. The pilot's cockpit was to the port side of the fuselage. (H Woodman)
▼

Numerical key

1. Looking down into front cockpit showing internal structure. The hinged portion of the gun ring is seen bottom right. 2. Close-up view of forward gun ring. The main ring, a heavy wooden structure, was fixed, the gun assembly actually running around a circular rail fitted to the top. The long diagonal bracing tube perforated to save weight pivoted on the cockpit floor. To bring the gun to rest it was drawn back so that the butt rested in the receiver seen on the support. The spigot was probably used to allow some kind of quick lashing around the butt to hold it in place. 3. View into front cockpit looking aft. Many things apparent here, including the side window (blacked out), the bomb release keys to the left of the window (each given different colours for the different racks), the cut-away bulkhead and, beyond this, the large window on the starboard side only, in this case not blacked out. The circular depression on the floor of the cockpit was to contain the reel for the trailing wireless aerial wire when fitted, whilst to the right can be seen an open access to the rear of the pilot's dashboard and below this the folding seat. 4. View looking back and over the rear gunner's cockpit. Note position of side screens (made from expanded metal not wire mesh), the large clip rest to the left to receive the gun butt, the semi-circular rails, the top cut out and the cut-away rear lower fuselage. The lower gun socket can be seen and to the bottom of the picture the canted former with the large circular cut-out. 5. Bracket fitted to fuselage to attach the centre section struts. 6. Front of back rack. Note the small bobbin shaped object on the right: this is a switch which causes a small light to go on in the front cockpit when the bomb is successfully released. 7. Main rib, the web of which is of plywood, extensively perforated, and the flange of solid wood grooved to fit upon the web to which it is tacked. 8. Junction of the two upper wing halves, showing steel wedge which fitted into staples as shown. 9. Joint used in lower wing structure looking from underneath the wing. The wire seen to the right is part of the internal bracing of the wing structure. 10. Close-up of joint box at spar end of wing. 11. Interplane strut joints. The struts themselves were of steel tube covered with a three-ply streamlined fairing. 12. Undercarriage detail. Note that the axle slides in a 'U' guide and its movement is controlled by two long compression springs contained within the main undercarriage struts. A strong steel cable passes over the top of the axle and then down under two pulleys contained at the top of the 'V', the spindles of which can be seen in the drawing. The cable then travels up inside the two legs and inside the long springs to the heads of adjustable bolts, to which the upper ends of the springs are fixed. The forward leg of the undercarriage only is covered with a three-ply fairing, whilst a similar but larger fairing is fitted to the axle as shown. This was held in place by three light straps and invariably hung down when the machine was on the ground. The outer ends had a 'T' piece which slotted in a cut-out in the 'V' and its purpose, according to the British report, was to prevent the axle turning out of alignment. 13. Sketch of tailskid. At its upper end it is fixed with loops of steel coil springs to two tubular steel rings clipped to each side of the fuselage. Note heavy steel shoe and bracing structure. The lower tail bracing struts are seen here, and an interesting point is that, on this particular machine at any rate, small spikes are fitted, apparently to prevent ground crew picking the tail up at an unbraced point. 14. Radiator showing shutter system. There was at least one other type of shutter, involving a sliding panel. 15, 16. Detail of engine bearers and joints. 17. Small control fitted each side of pilot's compartment controlling position of radiator shutters. 18. Throttle controls fitted to left of pilot (see drawing of dashboard) – one lever for each engine; the third was presumably to control both in one movement, but this is not known for certain. 19. Control column and wheel controlling ailerons fixed at the bottom to the transverse rod to which the elevator quadrants were fitted on the outside of the fuselage. 20. Elevator quadrants were of two types; this shows one type. The spokes were sometimes covered with fabric but usually left bare. The double cable controlling the ailerons can be seen leading from inside the transverse tubular piece. 21. Control tap for petrol (see dashboard). The three positions marked are for hand pump, motor pump and priming. 22. Method of fitting cables to rudder post. The elevator cables were also duplicated. 23. Contemporary drawing of GV dashboard. Note cutaway bulkhead at right and throttle control at left (area cut down to show). Pump at bottom right of dashboard is an air hand pump for the upper wing tank. Fuel controls are aluminium finish. Control column is omitted for clarity, and compass – normally placed at lower left of column – is also absent.

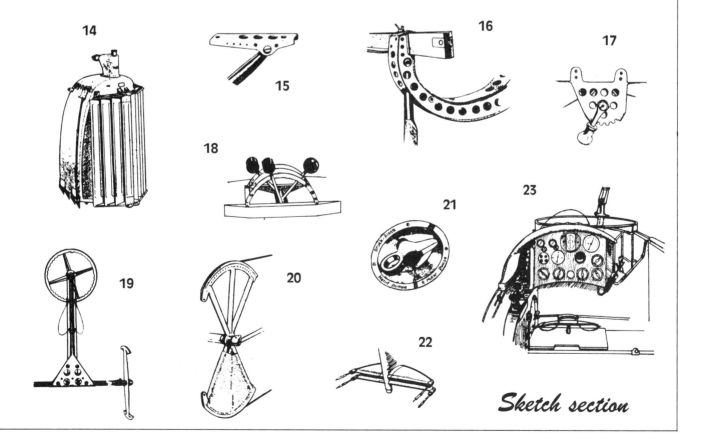

14 15 16 17 18 19 20 21 22 23

Sketch section

LVG C VI

Country of origin: Germany.
Type: Two-seat reconnaissance and artillery observation aircraft.
Powerplant: One Benz Bz IV six-cylinder, liquid-cooled engine rated at 200hp.
Dimensions: Wing span 42ft 8in *13.00m*; length 24ft 5¼in *7.45m*; height 9ft 2¼in

2.80m; wing area 372.4 sq ft *34.6m²*.
Weights: Empty 2050lb *930kg*; loaded 2886lb *1309kg*.
Performance: Maximum speed 105.5mph *170kph*; time to 3280ft *1000m*, 4min; service ceiling 21,325ft *6500m*; endurance 3.5hr.

Armament: One fixed Spandau machine gun and one flexibly mounted Parabellum machine gun, plus up to 250lb *113kg* of bombs.
Service: First flight early 1918; service entry summer 1918.

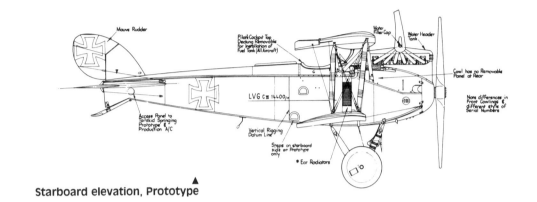

Starboard elevation, Prototype

The single fixed Spandau gun firing forward on the starboard side gave the LVG C VI some advantage, but it was no match for Camels or SE5s, two of which latter shot this sole survivor down on 2 August 1918. (R Moulton)

DRAWN BY MAURICE BRETT

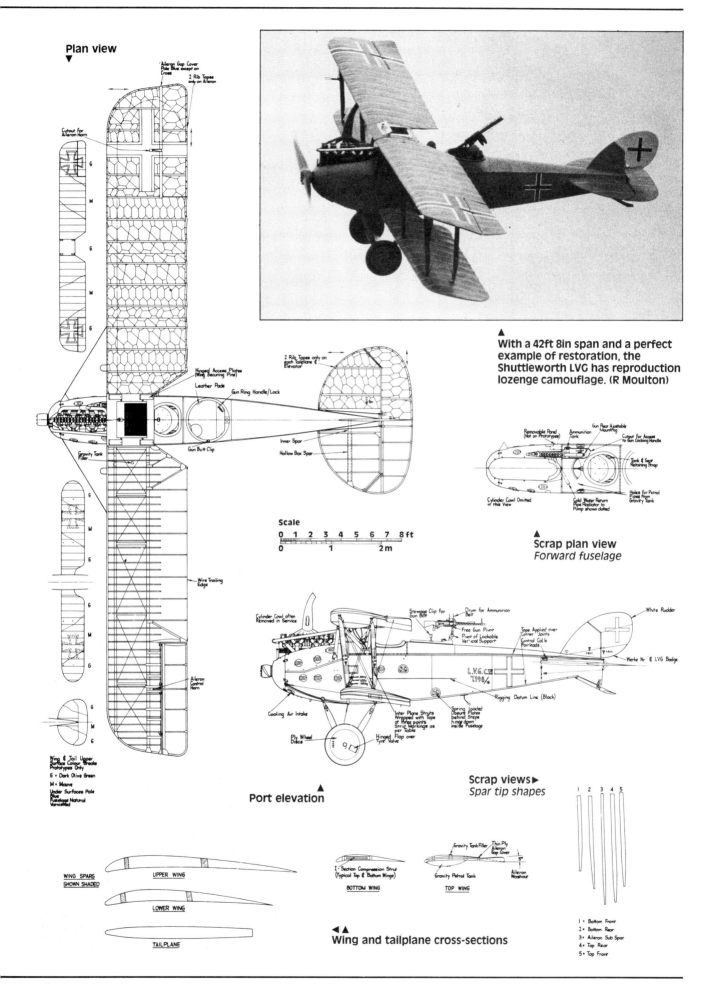

Plan view ▼

Aileron Gap Cover Pale Blue except on Cross

2 Rib Tapes only on Aileron

Cutout for Aileron Horn

Hinged Access Plates (Wing Securing Pins)

Leather Pads

Gun Ring Handle/Lock

Gun Butt Clip

Gravity Tank Filler

2 Rib Tapes only on each tailplane & Elevator

Inner Spar

Hollow Box Spar

Wire Trailing Edge

Aileron Control Horn

Wing & Tail Upper Surfaces Colour Breaks Prototypes Only

G = Dark Olive Green
M = Mauve

Under Surfaces Pale Blue Fuselage Natural Varnished

Port elevation ▲

▲ With a 42ft 8in span and a perfect example of restoration, the Shuttleworth LVG has reproduction lozenge camouflage. (R Moulton)

Removable Panel (Not on Prototypes)

Ammunition Tank

Gun Rear Adjustable Mounting

Cutout for Access to Gun Locking Handle

Tank & Seat Retaining Strap

Holes for Petrol Pipes from Gravity Tank

Cylinder Cowl Omitted in This View

Cold Water Return Pipe Radiator to Pump shown dotted

▲ **Scrap plan view**
Forward fuselage

Scale

| 0 | 1 | 2 | 3 | 4 | 5 | 6 | 7 | 8 ft |

| 0 | | 1 | | 2m |

Cylinder Cowl often Removed in Service

Stowage Clip for Gun Belt

Drum for Ammunition Belt

Free Gun Pivot
Pivot of Lockable Vertical Support

Tape Applied over Corner Joints

Control Cable Fairleads

White Rudder

Werke Nr & LVG Badge

L.V.G. C⟨?⟩
T196/4

Rigging Datum Line (Black)

Cooling Air Intake

Ply Wheel Discs

Inter Plane Struts Wrapped with Tape at three points Strut Markings as per Table

Spring Loaded Closure Plates behind Steps hinge down inside the Fuselage

Hinged Flap over Tyre Valve

Scrap views ▶
Spar tip shapes

WING SPARS SHOWN SHADED

UPPER WING

LOWER WING

TAILPLANE

I - Section Compression Strut (Typical Top & Bottom Wings)

BOTTOM WING

Gravity Tank Filler
Thin Ply Aileron Gap Cover

Gravity Petrol Tank

TOP WING

Aileron Washout

1 2 3 4 5

1 = Bottom Front
2 = Bottom Rear
3 = Aileron Sub Spar
4 = Top Rear
5 = Top Front

◀▲ **Wing and tailplane cross-sections**

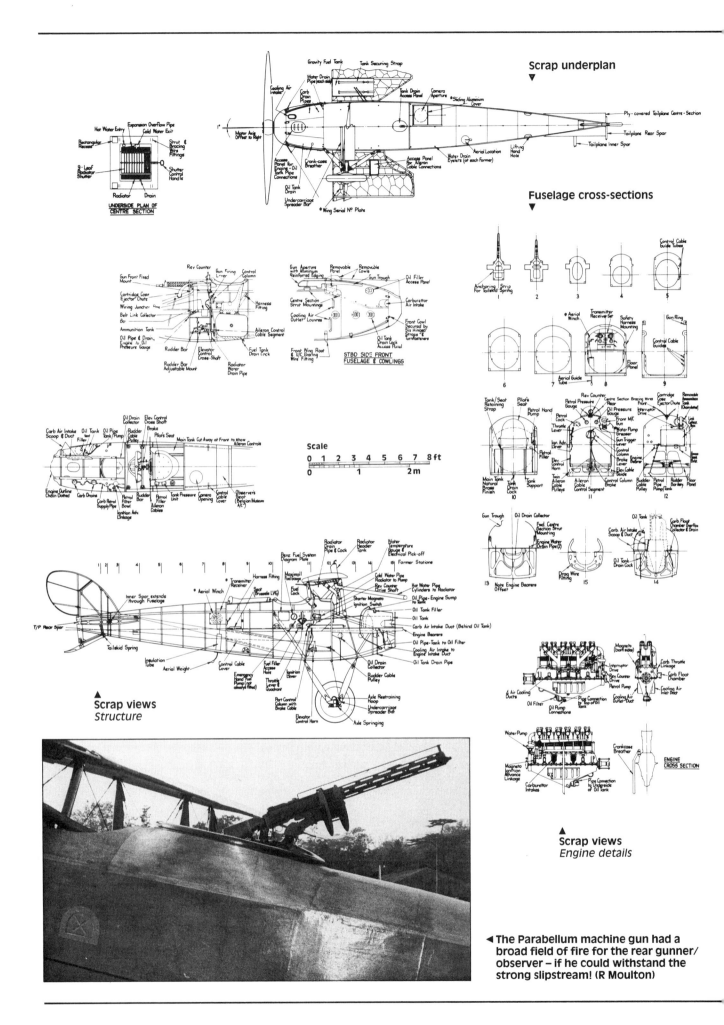

Scrap underplan ▼

UNDERSIDE PLAN OF CENTRE SECTION

Fuselage cross-sections ▼

STBD SIDE FRONT FUSELAGE & COWLINGS

scale

0 1 2 3 4 5 6 7 8 ft
0 1 2 m

▲ **Scrap views**
Structure

▲ **Scrap views**
Engine details

◄ The Parabellum machine gun had a broad field of fire for the rear gunner/observer – if he could withstand the strong slipstream! (R Moulton)

The 230hp Benz six-cylinder engine in the LVG C VI still runs well, albeit a trifle hot, for the Shuttleworth displays at Old Warden. (R Moulton)▶

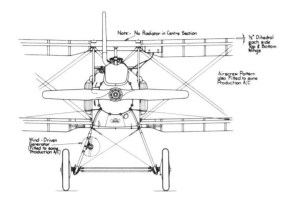

Note:- No Radiator in Centre Section

½° Dihedral each side Top & Bottom Wings

Airscrew Pattern also Fitted to some Production A/C

Wind-Driven Generator (Fitted to some Production A/C)

▲ **Scrap front elevation, Prototype**

Scale

0 1 2 3 4 5 6 7 8 ft

0   1   2m

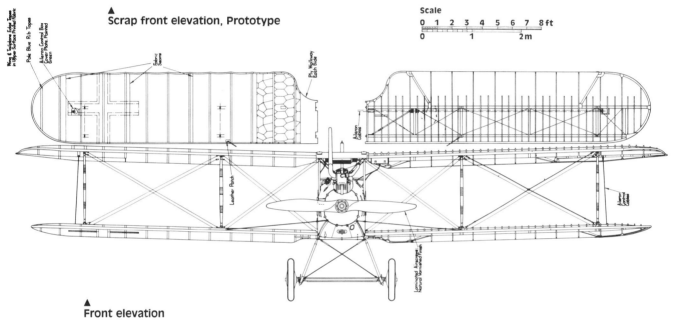

Wing & Tailplane Edge Tapes in Upper Surface Printed Fabric

Pale Blue Rib Tapes

Aileron Control Box Cover Plate Painted Green

Fabric Seams

Ply Walkway Each Side

Aileron Cables

Leather Patch

Laminated Airscrew Natural Varnished Finish

Aileron Cables

▲ **Front elevation**

Colour notes

All engine cowlings and metal panels on fuselage, struts, wheel discs, rev counter and control cable fairleads – light milk chocolate brown or light grey-green. Strut end fittings, tailskid fittings, control horns, all internal metal fittings, engine parts not cast alloy, serial and *Werke* number – semi-matt black. Centre section, all metal panels on wings, gravity tank, ply panels at lower wing roots, leather patches on fabric round control horns and fittings and tailplane rear spar – dark green. Fuselage and fin, tailplane centre-section, airscrew and gun ring (mahogany) – high-gloss varnished wood. Radiator – dull aluminium.

TABLE OF COLOURS		
Key	Munsell Code	Approximate Colour Description
	Upper	
1	10B2/2	Blue - Black
2	5P3/2	Dk Greyish-Purple
3	10YR5/4	Khaki - Yellow
4	10GY5/4	Sage - Green
5	5PB3/7	Dk Cobalt Blue
	Lower	
1	10G5/2	Lt Turquoise
2	10P5/2	Dk Mauve
3	10YR6/6	Golden Yellow
4	5RP5/6	Purplish Pink
5	2·5PB5/4	Blue - Grey

Basic Printed Fabric Pattern

Pattern Repeated in Direction of Arrow

• **Note**
Annotations Marked With ● Indicate Items Shape or Position Not Fully Authenticated

Black Cross with White Outline. No Black Line Round White.

Primrose Yellow Stars & LVG

French Blue Background

LVG BADGE

Light Brown Outline

Size of Upper & Lower Wing Crosses (Prototype Only)

 4503
FORM OF STENCIL Nºs FOR WERKE Nº

STRUT MARKINGS			
Left	Front	Outer	LVA
"	"	Inner	LVI
"	Rear	Outer	LHA
"	"	Inner	LHI
Right	Front	Outer	RVA
"	"	Inner	RVI
"	Rear	Outer	RHA
"	"	Inner	RHI

L.V.G. C.VI
7631/18

Style of Fuselage Serial No. (Werke Nr. 4586)

Position of Front Bulkhead (No.12)

 Rigging Diagram

Leergewicht 950 Kg
Nutzlast 430 Kg
Gesamtgewicht 1380 Kg

Rigging diagram & weights table 3 times scale

◀ **Scrap views**
Markings details

Roland D II

Country of origin: Germany.
Type: Single-seat scout.
Powerplant: One Mercedes D III six-cylinder, liquid-cooled engine rated at 160hp.
Dimensions: Wing span 29ft 4in *8.94m*;

length 22ft 8¾in *6.93m*; height 10ft 2½in *3.11m*; wing area 245.4 sq ft *22.8m²*.
Weights: Empty 1577lb *715kg*; loaded 2104lb *954kg*.
Performance: Maximum speed 105.5mph *170kph*; time to 16,400ft

5000m, 23min.
Armament: Two fixed Spandau machine guns.
Service: First flight October 1916.

DRAWN BY IAN R STAIR

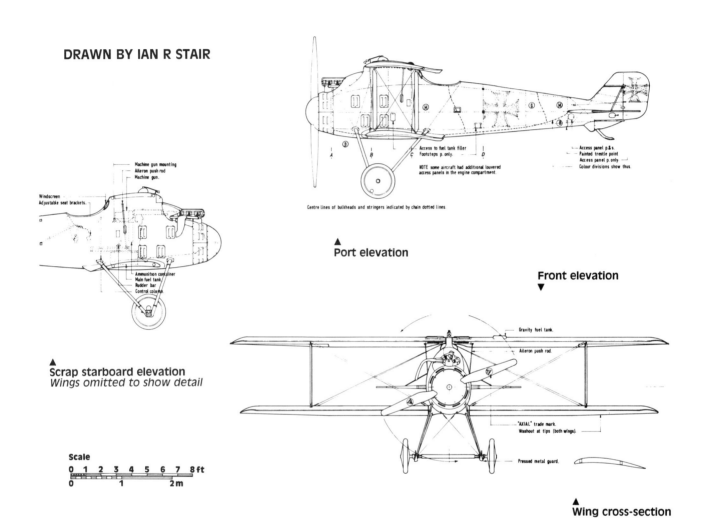

▲ **Port elevation**

▲ **Scrap starboard elevation**
Wings omitted to show detail

Front elevation ▼

▲ **Wing cross-section**

Scale

Colour notes
Top surfaces in dark green ('G') and mauve ('M') camouflage, the pattern of which varied. A typical scheme is shown. Undersurfaces light blue ('B'). Colours were oversprayed to give a misty edge. Position and size of crosses also varied.

◄ **A Roland D II marked with personal insignia at the cockpit. Despite its clean appearance, this aircraft had a poor handling performance and was unpopular. (H Woodman)**

▲
The Roland D II, powered by the 160hp Mercedes D III engine, appeared at the same time as the Albatros D III but was built in far lesser numbers: the 97 at the Front in April 1917 had dwindled to 10 by August. (A Imrie)

Plan view
▼

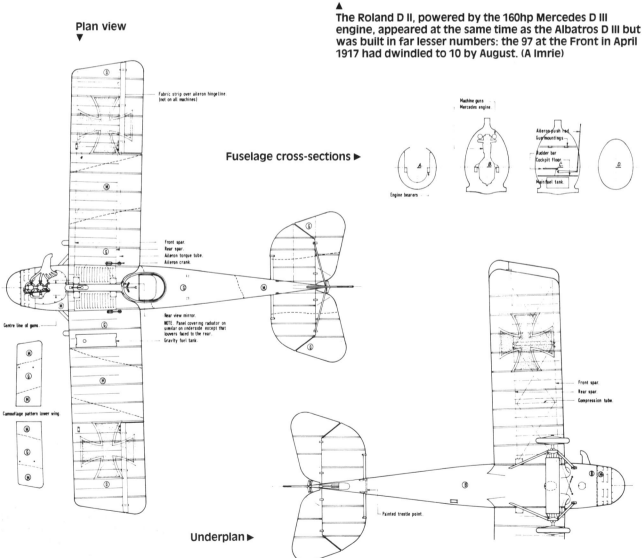

Fabric strip over aileron hinge line.
(not on all machines)

Fuselage cross-sections ▶

Machine guns
Mercedes engine.

Aileron push rod.
Gun mountings.

Rudder bar.
Cockpit floor.

Main fuel tank.

Engine bearers.

A

B

C

D

Front spar.
Rear spar.
Aileron torque tube.
Aileron crank.

Rear view mirror.
NOTE. Panel covering radiator on similar on underside except that louvers faced to the rear.
Gravity fuel tank.

Centre line of guns.

Camouflage pattern lower wing.

Front spar.
Rear spar.
Compression tube.

Painted trestle point.

Underplan ▶

Rumpler C IV

Country of origin: Germany.
Type: Two-seat reconnaissance aircraft.
Powerplant: One Mercedes D IVa six-cylinder, liquid-cooled engine rated at 260hp.
Dimensions: Wing span 41ft 6½in *12.66m*; length 27ft 7in *8.41m*; height 10ft 8in *3.25m*; wing area 360.6 sq ft *33.5m²*.
Weights: Empty 2381lb *1080kg*; 3374lb *1530kg*.
Performance: Maximum speed 106mph *170.5kph* at 1640ft *500m*; time to 1640ft, 2min; service ceiling 21,000ft *6400m*; endurance 3.5–4hr.
Armament: One fixed Spandau machine gun and one flexibly mounted Parabellum machine gun, plus up to four 55lb *25kg* bombs.
Service: Service entry 1917.

DRAWN BY IAN R STAIR

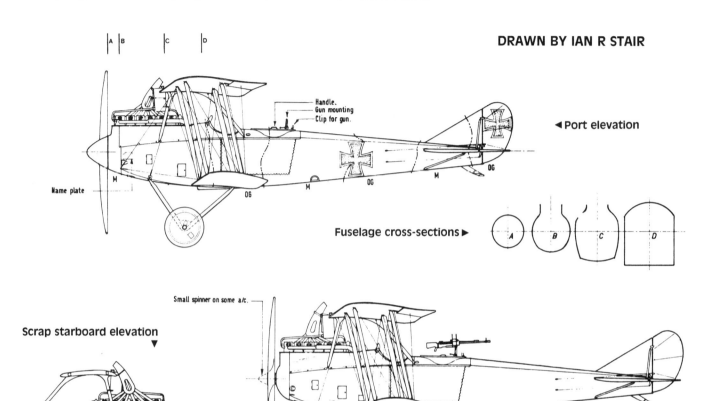

◄ Port elevation

Handle.
Gun mounting
Clip for gun.

Name plate

Fuselage cross-sections ►

Scrap starboard elevation ▼

Small spinner on some a/c.

▲
Port elevation, Late model
Note absence of spinner

Scale
0 1 2 3 4 5 6 7 8 ft
0   1   2m

◄ The Rumpler C IV, powered by the 260hp Mercedes D IVa six-cylinder engine, was a two-seater used for long range high-altitude photographic reconnaissance. Over 200 machines of this type were in service by the end of 1917. (A Imrie)

Colour notes
Typical colour scheme is shown on drawings. OG – Olive green; M – Mauve. Outlines were hazy, and brown was sometimes used in place of mauve. Undersurfaces and all struts were very pale blue.

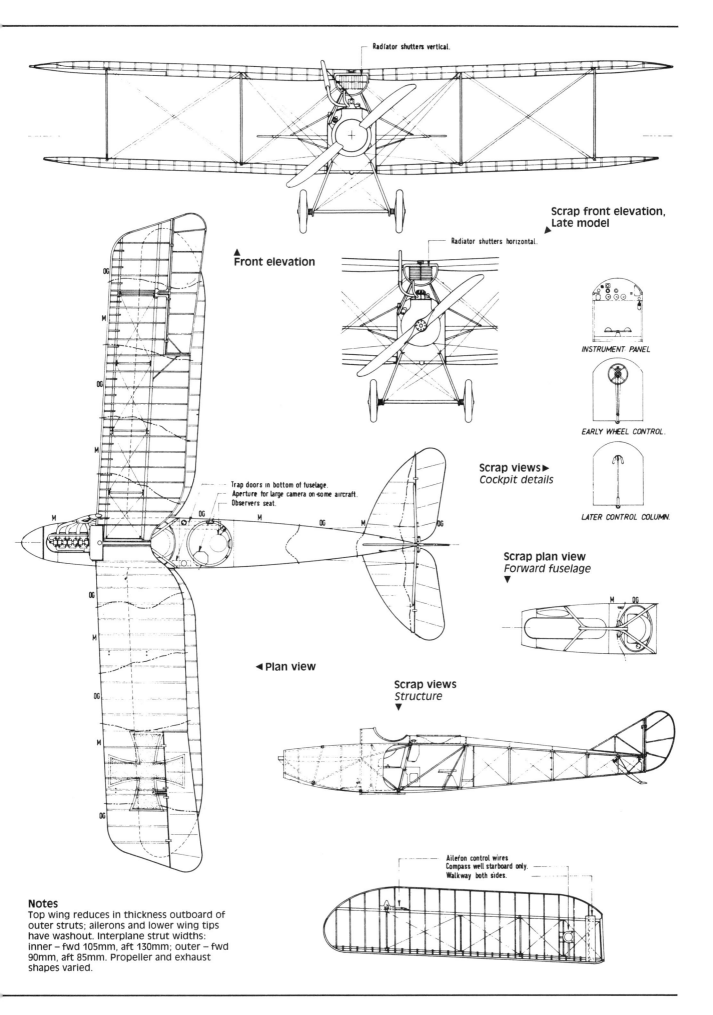

Radiator shutters vertical.

Scrap front elevation,
Late model

▲
Front elevation

Radiator shutters horizontal.

INSTRUMENT PANEL

EARLY WHEEL CONTROL.

LATER CONTROL COLUMN.

Scrap views►
Cockpit details

— Trap doors in bottom of fuselage.
— Aperture for large camera on some aircraft.
— Observers seat.

Scrap plan view
Forward fuselage
▼

◄**Plan view**

Scrap views
Structure
▼

Aileron control wires
Compass well starboard only.
Walkway both sides.

Notes
Top wing reduces in thickness outboard of
outer struts; ailerons and lower wing tips
have washout. Interplane strut widths:
inner – fwd 105mm, aft 130mm; outer – fwd
90mm, aft 85mm. Propeller and exhaust
shapes varied.

The Publisher wishes to thank the
following draughtsmen whose drawings
appear in this volume

MAURICE BRETT   P L GRAY
PETER G COOKSLEY   E J RIDING
GEORGE COX   IAN R STAIR
            HARRY WOODMAN